"This book is an imp
biblical counseling. W(
hensive approach to such issues as anxiety and panic disorders,
trauma, depression, and narcissism, where God 'speaks to every
square inch of life.' Too often, we address these issues in a piece-
meal fashion and relegate God to the sidelines, but Welch challenges us to listen to God, engage his Word, seek support from
the community of faith, and listen to and continually learn from
the experience of others, particularly in terms of the benefits
and limitations of medical and physical treatments. All problems have a deep and profound spiritual component, and all
caregiving should respond in terms of both the immediate issue
and the eternal consequences. Highly recommended for pas-
tors, counselors, and people ministering to or dealing with such
difficult and complex issues."

> **Ian F. Jones,** Professor of Counseling, Associate Dean, Divi-
> sion of Counseling, Baptist Community Ministries' Chair
> of Pastoral Counseling, New Orleans Baptist Theological
> Seminary

"Psychiatric diagnosis defines much suffering today but can
feel off-limits for churches. In this book, complex problems are
masterfully distilled into biblical categories. Ed also imparts a
humble confidence: humility to hear wisdom crying out in the
psychological world and confidence to give God's wisdom the
final word. This book advances my counseling and invites a
hesitant church to care wisely."

> **Dr. Andrew Collins,** Consultant Psychiatrist, NHS, UK;
> biblical counsellor and tutor, Biblical Counselling UK

"I usually turn first to Ed Welch when I want to better grasp
the spiritual dimension of the embodied soul. Here Ed gives us a
robust and helpful accounting of our spiritual nature in situations
when most only speak of our brains run amok. He shows us how
the gospel speaks wisdom into every inch of God's creation, how
psychiatric disorders are fully spiritual problems as well as physical, and how the gospel provides the hope we need."

> **Dr. John Applegate,** Executive Director of JA&A and the
> Philadelphia Renewal Network

"Written eloquently, Ed Welch shows us why the gospel matters for all of life, including psychiatric diagnoses. Whether it's related to trauma or depression, he provides biblical wisdom that strengthens our trust in Jesus with practical guidance along the way. This book is hope-filled because the gospel is central."

**Lilly Park,** Associate Professor, Southwestern Baptist Theological Seminary

"Although psychiatric diagnoses are an important tool to identify important human struggles, Ed Welch effectively considers how the Bible helps us see beyond the struggles to a deeper and better hope. Effective medical treatments are necessary, but our peace and hope can only be found in Jesus Christ and the gospel. Nothing on earth completely rescues us from death or brings true peace."

**Eduardo Saladin,** Pastor, Sola Gratia Biblical Church, Dominican Republic; certified biblical counselor, ACBC; board member, CCEF

"This is a book full of biblical wisdom, written with a biblical counselor's heart for those searching for biblical answers. If you or someone you know has a psychiatric symptom or diagnosis, this book will help you find wisdom, rest, and hope in Jesus through Scripture."

**Dr. Chris Schofield,** Consultant Psychiatrist, NHS, UK; involved in biblical counselling in the local church

"This is an accessible and much-needed resource written as much for those providing spiritual care as it is for those dealing with psychiatric diagnoses themselves. Ed Welch helps us appreciate the real struggles described by several common disorders while also showing pathways for spiritual growth in the midst of those struggles."

**Ben Lyon,** Executive Pastor, Trinity Presbyterian Church, Norfolk, VA

"As a psychiatrist my *safar* (journey) started with this question: is there a divide between psychiatry and spirituality? Are they friends or foes? Dr. Welch has broken the walls of the illusionary divide in this book. Who are we? We are embodied souls before God. Thank you, Ed, for writing this guidebook for everyone who embarks on that journey."

**Dr. Raja Paulraj,** Psychiatrist and Counselor, Landour Community Hospital, India

"When I'm looking for balanced thoughtfulness with counseling issues, I regularly turn to Ed Welch. Once again, he's provided a valuable resource for the challenging issues faced by hurting people. This book charts a course through the most common psychiatric diagnoses with compassion, grace, and biblical truth. In a world of 'either-or,' Welch offers a wealth of wisdom. I'm grateful for this practical and timely book!"

**Mark Vroegop,** Lead Pastor of College Park Church, Indianapolis, IN; author of *Dark Clouds, Deep Mercy: Discovering the Grace of Lament*

"When I was previously diagnosed with a mental disorder, it felt like my entire world was being redefined. I struggled to find biblical resources that spoke to my lived experiences in an approachable way. This book is what I needed to read in those early days. It gently addresses common questions, empathizes with the sufferer's nuanced problems, and offers practical encouragement for walking forward with Jesus on a challenging post-diagnosis journey."

**Christine Chappell,** Author of *Help! I've Been Diagnosed with a Mental Disorder*; outreach director and *Hope + Help Podcast* host, Institute for Biblical Counseling & Discipleship; certified biblical counselor

"Diagnostic categories can either seem competitive with biblical understanding or used to justify inexcusable behavior. Ed Welch clearly explains the meaning behind common psychiatric diagnoses and brilliantly offers redemptive and restorative perspective to address these maladies. His championing of biblical categories doesn't create a false divide between biblical wisdom and psychological reflection. Instead he irenically brings the lens of Scripture to intensify our need for Jesus."

**Dan B. Allender,** Professor of Counseling Psychology, The Seattle School of Theology and Psychology

"Ed Welch has tackled this delicate and challenging area of the Christian life with characteristic wisdom and kindness. He walks closely to Scripture and to Christ and shows rich, nourishing connections with anxiety and panic attacks, depression, and trauma. This will feed the soul—for sufferer and carer/counselor—over the long haul, with many short sentences of distilled, sweet grace. The final chapter breaks glorious new ground, teaching and modeling love, grace, and understanding for people with narcissistic qualities. If narcissism is a problem of our age, then this book offers Jesus and his gospel to his people in new ways we most desperately need."

**Andrew Nicholls,** Director of Pastoral Care, Oak Hill College, London, UK; coauthor of *Real Change*

# I HAVE A
# PSYCHIATRIC
# DIAGNOSIS

## WHAT DOES THE BIBLE SAY?

## Edward T. Welch

New
Growth
Press

newgrowthpress.com

New Growth Press, Greensboro, NC 27401
newgrowthpress.com

Cover Design: Studio Gearbox, studiogearbox.com
Interior Design and Typesetting: Gretchen Logterman

ISBN: 978-1-64507-280-5 (Print)
ISBN: 978-1-64507-281-2 (eBook)

Library of Congress Cataloging-in-Publication Data
Names: Welch, Edward T., 1953- author.
Title: I have a psychiatric diagnosis : what does the Bible say? / Edward
    T. Welch.
Description: Greensboro, NC : New Growth Press, [2022] | Series: Ask the
    Christian counselor | Includes bibliographical references and index. |
    Summary: "Edward T. Welch helps you answer questions by exploring how
    God's Word speaks in ways that can help you find wisdom, rest, and hope
    in Jesus, even with a psychiatric diagnosis"-- Provided by publisher.
Identifiers: LCCN 2022015620 (print) | LCCN 2022015621 (ebook) | ISBN
    9781645072805 (print) | ISBN 9781645072812 (ebook)
Subjects: LCSH: Mental illness--Biblical teaching. |
    Christianity--Psychology. | Psychiatry and religion. | Mental
    health--Biblical teaching. | Pastoral psychology. | Pastoral counseling.
Classification: LCC BT732.4 .W45 2022 (print) | LCC BT732.4 (ebook) | DDC
    261.8/322--dc23/eng/20220414
LC record available at https://lccn.loc.gov/2022015620
LC ebook record available at https://lccn.loc.gov/2022015621

Printed in the United States of America

29 28 27 26 25 24 23 22      1 2 3 4 5

# CONTENTS

# INTRODUCTION

I remember the first time I witnessed the partition between God's words and the psychological world. My wife and I were visiting a family from our church, and their eight-year-old son answered the door. He was by himself. He appeared confident around adults, not shy. Obviously schooled in manners.

"Hi," he said, "I'm Johnny. I have ADHD."

I had no idea how to reply. I briefly considered, "Hi Johnny-with-ADHD." Then "I'm Ed. I have ____," but I couldn't locate a fitting self-diagnosis on the spot. So I settled for, "Hi, Johnny, are your parents home?"

As I came to know him and the family, his introduction made sense. I could understand why ADHD had such a high profile in the home. But they never breached the divide between the diagnosis and "What does God say?" As a family they never seemed to consider that the gospel of Jesus Christ could speak even more deeply than his diagnosis of ADHD. Since then I have noticed that for many thoughtful followers of Jesus, when they take psychiatric medication, Jesus is part of Sunday but is largely absent from the struggles that can feel so life dominating.

What I have tried to do in this small book is take Scripture at its word. God speaks to everything. He is certainly familiar with the many types of struggles we can face. Whatever the trouble might be, he still assures us that his life can break in and make our life more abundant. The more we have of him, the more we are strengthened in all our troubles. The more we respond by faith—with the help of many people—the more hope grows and the more Jesus takes the center. We get to see how everything is beautifully folded into him, as with gentleness and affection, he says, "Mine."

# Chapter 1

## BRIDGING THE DIVIDE

Right now you are here: panic disorder, depression, anorexia, obsessive-compulsive personality disorder, attention-deficit/hyperactivity disorder, trauma, substance abuse, bipolar disorder. You are carrying a heavy burden—you or someone you love has a psychiatric diagnosis.

You want to find your way to here:

- What does God say?
- How does the Bible speak in ways that can help you find wisdom, rest, and hope in Jesus, even with a psychiatric diagnosis?

That path is not always easy. It's as if there are walls between psychological problems and God's words. Therapists and psychiatrists don't talk about God; Scripture doesn't have a list of psychological diagnoses. Two different worlds. One science, the other spiritual. Maybe they each have their own areas of expertise and don't need to be bridged. Maybe?

Still, we have to do *something*. The troubles described by psychiatric diagnoses are life dominating. They can be our most pressing problems. It just doesn't make sense that God is relatively silent on something so important.

3

And we know he is not silent. God, we can be sure, hears and has compassion for us in this pain. Hear his words to us: "As one whom his mother comforts, so I will comfort you" (Isaiah 66:13a). He is the "God of all comfort" who comforts in a way that our comfort can even overflow to others (2 Corinthians 1:3–4). He is the Lord whose comfort brings peace in all kinds of troubles. (The evidence for Scripture's words to suffering people is the hundreds of fine books on suffering. A sample of these appears at the end of the book.)

Jesus says, "I have told you these things, so that in me you may have peace. In this world you will have trouble. But take heart! I have overcome the world" (John 16:33, NIV). We know that when Jesus says "overcome" he does not mean complete physical healing and the eradication of all trouble in this life. But he does mean that the life he has given us will reach into the darkness we so often feel (John 10:10), and hope will push back despair.

Do you have doubts about this? Jesus responds to those doubts. He promises—he even swears—that he gives us his presence and power because of what he has done in his death and resurrection (Matthew 28:20). Still have your doubts? He gently points to well-fed birds and colorful daylilies. God cares for them, he says. "Are you not of more value than they?" (Matthew 6:26). If God knows the details of common birds and flowers, which can last only a day, he certainly knows and cares about what troubles you. If comfort seems slow to come, he invites you to ask, "When will you comfort me?" (Psalm 119:82). He will certainly hear you and will bring comfort and much more.

What you need is for these truths to break into your psychological struggles. Your well-being and spiritual growth are at stake.

Notice what occurs with a word such as *trauma*. You think about chronic abuse or a gruesome event that etched an indelible mark of death on someone's mind and body. Those past events intrude into present life, as if they *are* present. Sometimes they intrude as vivid flashbacks. A mere scent, a noise, a word, a scene in a movie, and your body abruptly shuts down and hopes to numb you from the threat. When you want help, your thoughts might go to relaxation techniques, mindfulness, and careful attention to your breathing, though you would settle for staying alive through the storm.

What you *do not* think is what God says about trauma. Since the word *trauma* doesn't appear in Scripture, it seems as though he has little to say about it. His words are *spiritual*, and spiritual resides in a different world than *psychological problems*. Spiritual, we think, is about heaven. It is for later, not now.

## PSYCHOLOGICAL AND SPIRITUAL

Just a word on the terms *psychological* and *spiritual*. *Psychological* and *psychiatric problems* are often used interchangeably. They refer to disruptive thoughts and feelings that interfere with our relationships, growth, and work. They typically assume that both our bodies and the destructive acts of other people are the primary causes. Many of these difficult experiences have been catalogued in the *Diagnostic and Statistical Manual of Mental Disorders* (*DSM–5*) of the American Psychiatric Association.[1] They include depressive disorders, bipolar, anxiety, schizophrenia, trauma, and many others. *Psychiatric* suggests that medication might be used as a treatment. *Psychological* promotes nonmedical strategies to manage emotions, revise hazardous thought patterns, and direct the course of relationships.

These terms have been contrasted with *spiritual problems*. If we have a spiritual problem, we usually think that we are supposed to read our Bible and pray. Or, perhaps we are hard-hearted and rebellious, and our heavenly future could be in jeopardy. With that perspective, psychological and spiritual problems dwell in two different worlds because psychological problems cannot be reduced to a rebellious heart or cured by mere spiritual disciplines. Scripture, however, suggests that *spiritual* is much more than these.

Scripture speaks to both the physical and relationally traumatic causes that are of prime interest in psychological and psychiatric problems. God has created us physical beings, and Scripture certainly accounts for body and brain disabilities that inevitably affect us all. God speaks about our bodies. Watch for the word *weak* as a common way that Scripture refers to physical struggles. For example, "The spirit indeed is willing, but the flesh [i.e., the body] is *weak*" (Mark 14:38, emphasis added). In other words, though we might intend to stay up late and pray, our bodies do not always cooperate with our good intentions. This means that, in our care for each other, we recognize that thoughts, feelings, and actions can be affected by our bodies, which could mean lack of sleep, strokes, the side effects of medication, and even all kinds of possible chemical or anatomical problems in the brain that presently avoid detection.

Scripture is also about our relationships: "Woe to the shepherds who destroy and scatter the sheep of my pasture!" declares the Lord (Jeremiah 23:1). Violence, in word and deed, destroys. God sees us when others have sinned against us, and God speaks to us when we have been victimized by violent acts. The occasion for many of the psalms is oppression and violence, in which the psalmists, speaking for us all, are at the end of themselves, and they turn to God for strength, help, and justice.

Spiritual problems go deep. They are matters of our spirit for which we need the Spirit. We might benefit from medication and other treatments, but we need God and his Spirit above all else. Let's consider this more carefully.

A spiritual problem has to do with your spirit. Your spirit is the real you—all things good, bad, confused, painful, uncertain, worth celebrating, your loves, your doubts, your shame, and whatever you hope to keep secret. You will notice other words substitute for *spirit*, such as *heart*, *mind*, and *soul* (*heart* is the most common). They all identify beliefs held most dearly, the emotions that express true desires, and the effects of broken relationships that seem to descend on every moment of life. They also identify the center of our being, in which life is lived before God and we need him. Spiritual problems extend more broadly than we first imagine.

In your spirit

- You can be crushed by the words of another (Proverbs 15:4).
- You need to be revived (Isaiah 57:15).
- You face emotions and desires that can control you, so you want to learn how to rule them more than be ruled by them (Proverbs 16:32).
- You can be deceived by your emotions. Sometimes you need to listen to them; other times they lie to you

about who you are—falsely saying that you are a hopeless case, you will never change, you will always feel this way, and no one cares (Proverbs 19:2).

- You can be much less secure than you let on, and wish there was someone whom you could trust and could actually help and protect (Luke 12:32).
- You can hate people who have wronged you and love them at the same time (Psalm 55:12–14).
- You wonder if God hears or sees or cares. You wonder if he is angry at you. You worry that he does not like you (Psalm 10:1).
- You don't need to know everything about tomorrow, but you do need help in how to live today (Psalm 25:4).
- You learn how you can be strong and alive even when your body and brain are imposing real hardships (Philippians 4:12–13).

In your spirit, you are also given power by the Spirit, who is the only one with access to your deepest thoughts and struggles, and who alone can truly help. Spiritual problems mean that you need God: Father, Son, and Spirit. Life is too much to manage on your own. You cannot afford to be partitioned from him. You could say that spiritual problems are reasons to pray—and you pray for everything, "but in everything by prayer and supplication with thanksgiving let your requests be made known to God" (Philippians 4:6).

Cancer, for example, is included in "everything." In the midst of medical treatments, we pray for healing and physical strength. *Spiritual* includes this and goes deeper yet. We are grateful for effective medical treatments, but we also know we cannot put our hope in them because nothing on earth wholly rescues us from death or brings peace. Cancer raises issues of life and death, purpose, endurance, the goodness of God, and life *after* death, and God's words go even to these places.

Spiritual deepens our understanding of psychological problems. The two categories are not actually opposed. Psychological categories help us see important human struggles. Spiritual categories include those struggles and help us see more. Spiritual indicates that God speaks in every detail of our lives, and we *need* him in every detail. Psychological therapies see fear and anxiety as an occasion to think differently—"I have no good reason to think that the bridge will fall when I am on it"—or dull the intense physical experiences through medication or other techniques that bring our attention to the present rather than the future. They cannot see that fear and anxiety need the right person, who is present, strong and trustworthy. They miss that we can put our trust in things and people (including ourselves) that cannot bear such confidence. They miss that we were created to be close to God, and, when the Spirit of God brings us close, everything changes.

## YOU ARE AN EMBODIED SOUL, NOT A PIE CHART

A common way to picture the difference between psychological and spiritual is they are two different pieces of a whole, the third piece being the physical, the realm of the body and brain. The psychological has laid claim to how we feel, how we think, how we live with others, and disruptions in any of these (fig. 1). The spiritual is left with obedience and hope for heaven, both of which can seem unrelated to psychological problems.

### Figure 1. A Common View of the Person

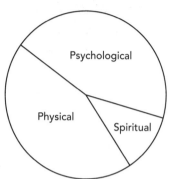

Now reimagine your theological x-ray. You are, indeed, a physical being, as represented by the circle in figure 2. Your body and brain are you, and they shape and influence both your feelings and thoughts. But your heart (spirit or soul) goes deeper. Here are your true desires, where you direct the course of your life. Here is where God gives life even when your body and brain are weakened or broken. Here is where peace, comfort, and hope can reside even during the complicated storms of life, or even storms of the brain and body. Here is where your God speaks to everything.

### Figure 2. The Embodied Soul

If we were to add more to this theological picture, we—body/spirit—are surrounded by a world that shapes us. It includes people and their impact, for good and bad, our work, our money, the culture in which we were raised, and an endless number of other influences. Even more, it includes spiritual beings, some who protect and others who have declared war (fig. 3).

### Figure 3. The Person and Examples of Life's Influences

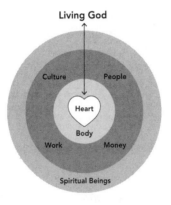

The Dutch theologian Abraham Kuyper described our life this way: "There is not a square inch in the whole domain of our human existence over which Christ, who is Sovereign over all, does not cry, Mine!" This means that we want to bring our psychological or psychiatric problems, which have been living apart from God's words, back to our home in Jesus Christ, and hear how he cares about the details of our lives. In this place he speaks hope to the depressed soul and rest to the anxious heart. He is the rock for those who feel like the present is overwhelming and confusing. From the vantage point of

God's kingdom, from where he says "Mine," everything is clearer and tinted with hope.

We will continue to gather reliable information and help from the world around us. Such help can have real benefits. Physical struggles might benefit from medical and physical treatments, and the consequences of broken relationships can be seen more clearly through the descriptions found in many good books. But, when God says "Mine," we gain everything as we reenvision our psychological problems. Careful observations, like those of the mental health sciences, help us to see important things; Scripture reveals what is *most* important. It opens our eyes to what is unseen and eternal.

## A PLAN

Here is our basic approach.

- Listen to God and get help from his people.
- Listen and learn from those who have experience.

Their order is not important, though we should always give God the final word.

Your work might begin when you learn something about a psychiatric diagnosis from those with experience. These sources can include friends, therapists, doctors, and reliable materials. You recognize yourself or someone you love in the descriptions—"OCD," "bipolar disorder," "borderline," and so on—and those words are important. They help you identify something for which you previously had no words. They might even bring a measure of relief. You feel known. "That's me." You finally feel understood. It is difficult to do anything until you put those hard-to-express experiences into speech.

What next? Listen to God. What does he say? What does *Scripture* say? These questions will remind you to bring what you have learned back to God's house, where you listen to him and his people. Here, the words you have heard in the world around you will be reshaped and you will see more. Scripture, it turns out, functions as corrective lenses that open your eyes.

These two approaches anchor the rhythm in what is ahead—listen to Scripture and God's people, listen to those who have experience, listen to what God says. Back-and-forth. Listen, learn, ask for help. The cycle continues until you understand your struggles (or another's struggles) better and have ways to help. What is important is that Scripture has the final words of hope.

## GOD'S WORDS TO YOU

There will be times when you bring what you have heard back to Scripture, and you hear nothing. At those times, here are words you can count on.

- Jesus says, "Speak to me."
- Jesus says, "Believe the gospel."

These will be your entrance into God's house.

### "Speak to Me"

When in doubt, start here. Life with God is an intimate and life-giving conversation. That's what you do in the best of human relationships. When something is hard, confusing or painful—when you experience trouble—you talk to a good friend, and Jesus calls his people friends (John 15:13–15).

That is *much* harder than it seems. We can speak to a good friend about our troubles. That is natural and even instinctive to our human nature. But it takes practice to talk to the Lord. We might ask for help when we are desperate, but we struggle to tell him the matters that are on our hearts. We don't know how to simply talk to him.

Try this: "Jesus, this is just so hard. I don't even know where to begin." Just talk. There are no particular rules. It is enough to know that Jesus listens and responds when you speak. He hears you and acts. You might not see him in action immediately, but you will.

"Pour out your heart," he says (Psalm 62:8). In response, his people have had plenty to say.

> For my soul is full of troubles,
>     and my life draws near to Sheol.
> I am counted among those who go down to the pit;
>     I am a man who has no strength,
> like one set loose among the dead. (Psalm 88:3–5a)

> Out of the depths I cry to you, O Lord. (Psalm 130:1)

*An idea:* When you talk about your present struggles, instead of using a technical term for whatever troubles you, such as *depression* or *bipolar*, use your own words and be as descriptive as you can. What is it like for you? What image captures it? Does it feel like darkness? Being taken hostage? Your body is a stranger? Think about what words you want to say, and then speak them to God and other people.

Your work has begun in earnest. A small but important step. You have taken a private pain or concern and made it public. You have openly expressed your need. Once you have done this with the Lord, you will notice that you can speak more freely to other people. You will speak similar words to a friend. You might ask someone to pray for you. When you speak from your heart to the Lord, conversations with other people are sure to follow, and God will use many of those conversations. The words and questions from other people will help you, and you, through your openness and willingness to talk to Jesus, will help them.

The Lord invites you to speak to him and his people, which will open the door to many more words he will speak. These words will cluster around, "Believe the gospel."

### "Believe the Gospel"

The apostle Paul summarizes the gospel this way: "Now I would remind you, brothers, of the gospel I preached to you. . . . For I delivered to you as of first importance what I also received: that Christ died for our sins in accordance with the Scriptures, that he was buried, that he was raised on the third day in accordance with the Scriptures" (1 Corinthians 15:1a, 3–4).

The gospel is a person. Jesus is the message that God has forgiven our sins because Jesus identified with us and died the death that we deserved so we could be brought close to God forever. This gospel is about the real us—our spirit—and about our suffering. From this beginning are all the benefits we have from being connected to Jesus, such as his comfort and power. Through this gospel we are changed by the Holy Spirit, who has been given to all who believe. His power can be found in those who have learned contentment, thankfulness, and even joy, although their circumstances did not improve. His power can be found in those who speak to him even when he seems far away, who love others even when they feel empty and lifeless. Whatever form that power takes, we could say the result of being filled with God's power is that his people are more alive. We are invited to press this gospel into every detail of our lives and watch his power enter into our weakness and pain.

All this follows an ancient tradition. The apostle Paul illustrated that pattern even to the first New Testament churches: "when I came to you . . . I decided to know nothing among you except Jesus Christ and him crucified" (1 Corinthians 2:1–2). This does not mean that his sermons were short, or that he answered every question, "Christ crucified." Paul means that Christ crucified, risen, and reigning is the heart of God's wisdom, so he committed himself to connecting every challenging detail of life to this center. Those connections are not always obvious to us, but a wise person searches for them because Jesus Christ is "the power of God and the wisdom of God" (1 Corinthians 1:24b). We will use that strategy.

For this work, we should get help from others who know people and know God. That is an essential part of God's plan. We learn in dependence on God and with other people's help. No human being is self-sufficient. Instead, we were intended to need one another. Henri Nouwen wrote of his own struggles, "I realized that healing begins with our taking our pain out of its diabolic isolation and seeing that whatever we suffer, we suffer it in communion with all of humanity."[2] In other words, we talk about our struggles with others. We are part of a multifaceted body, with each person bringing gifts that uniquely serve, and we need those gifts.

Then you broaden your search again. You talk to the world around you. You listen to those who have expertise in your particular problem. You ask questions. You learn from those who have *had* troubles like your own or seen troubles like your own. You listen, talk, ask. These can all contribute to your growth as you make it a point to always bring what you learn back to God's house where you hear his words.

Up ahead are four fairly common terms that come from psychiatry and psychotherapy: anxiety and panic disorder, trauma, depression, and narcissism. Each will bring its own particular challenges as you talk to the Lord and learn what he says to you in Scripture. The plan is that, once you develop the habit of returning to God's house and his words, you will be able to turn to him for meaningful help with all kinds of psychological—that is, spiritual—struggles.

## QUESTIONS FOR REFLECTION

1. Does the theological x-ray of the embodied soul make sense? It is one way to assemble a few biblical teachings into one diagram. The most important application of the embodied soul diagram is that God is in the center of everything. The rest of the book will illustrate how to see that God, indeed, is the center of our lives and the very center of our world.

2. The apostle Peter wrote, "His divine power has granted to us all things that pertain to life and

godliness" (2 Peter 1:3a). God's words say more than we will ever comprehend. How are you learning that in other areas of your life, such as in your relationships and your own daily troubles?

# Chapter 2

# ANXIETY AND PANIC DISORDERS

You are probably familiar with anxiety and panic disorders, or panic attacks. Because these problems are so common, they are a good place to begin. We will first consider some general observations about anxiety and panic, and then we will go to the question, What does God say? In Scripture, the Lord speaks to us in literally hundreds of passages that use the words *fear* or *anxiety*, but we will only land on a few of them.

## LISTEN AND LEARN FROM OTHERS

Our general observations about anxiety and panic begin with simple descriptions. Fear and anxiety signal that something important to you is threatened. The primary threats are to your money, your reputation, your relationships, and your health, or the well-being of those you love. Fear can usually identify a specific threat; anxiety notices a handful of threats swirling around with more and more threats joining them in their chaos. Panic attacks feel as though your very life is threatened. You have lost control of your mind and body. Think of it as internal anarchy.

Panic attacks usually come without any warning. They might reach their peak in only a few minutes, then the symptoms gradually subside; but the event leaves you shaken for hours—like aftershocks from a major earthquake—and you might notice the consequences long after. If you have had one, you will probably have another, which adds a layer of fear for when it might come again. Then the panic attacks, or the possibility of a panic attack, might make your world smaller. You don't go to the store where it first happened. You only drive on back roads. You avoid places that don't have an exit nearby. You cling to one person, and you avoid others. Your "world" shrinks to the size of your home.

Perhaps you have heard of the body's flight-or-fight response to threats. During panic attacks, your body chooses flight. You want to get out of wherever you are and get to a place where you can breathe. The diagnostic criteria are mostly physical symptoms. They include at least four of the following: accelerated heart rate, sweating, trembling, the feeling of being short of breath or choking, chest discomfort, nausea, feeling light-headed, feeling detached from the rest of the world, fear of losing control, fear of dying, numbness, chills, or hot flashes.

Because the physical symptoms are so intense, your first instinct is most likely to ask for help from a physician. Physical problems can contribute to panic attacks—heart conditions, caffeine intake, side effects from medications, and others. Some of these medical problems can actually trigger an attack. But don't be surprised if a physician offers what might seem to be a cursory exam and quickly gives a diagnosis of panic disorder that is unrelated to a treatable, medical condition. Most physicians have seen the symptoms of a panic attack many times before. That does not mean that the attacks are not real. It simply means that there is no clear medical problem that provokes them. You might leave the consultation with a prescription for antianxiety medication that can calm your body when an attack begins.

If you mention panic attacks to a sympathetic friend or if you read online material, you will receive advice on how to breathe, think less catastrophically, and be more optimistic. These can all be helpful. Your work would seem to be done. God, however, is missing, which suggests that your work is just beginning.

## LISTEN TO GOD AND HIS PEOPLE

When nudged toward God's words, you remember, "don't be anxious," which doesn't help. If anything, such words seem to lack insight into the experience of panic and may be a reason why you don't immediately turn to Scripture. Panic is outside of your control, and a reprimand to your anxious mind is ineffective at best. At worst, it adds a coating of guilt. But don't stop there. The gospel means "good news," which means that the words "don't be anxious" must be more encouraging than you think. Here is a rule of thumb: if it doesn't sound good, you have not yet arrived at the gospel—at Jesus.

### "Speak to Me"

Start with what you know. First, talk to Jesus. Gather words for your feelings, gather images, and talk to him. "I feel like there is something wrong with me. I wonder if I am going crazy." "What I went through . . . I thought my heart was going to burst. Or my mind would."

You could also borrow words spoken by psalmists.

> My heart is in anguish within me;
>> the terrors of death have fallen upon me.
> Fear and trembling come upon me,
>> and horror overwhelms me. (Psalm 55:4–5)

If we believe that our anxieties are simply to be commanded away, we do not speak them to the Lord. Why would we? He already told us not to be anxious. We should just speak to ourselves with a simple, "Stop it." Our fears and anxieties, however, are not that commandable. They need the right *person*, who is both strong and loving, who both hears us and speaks with us. Everything depends on having that right person.

Now go further in. Who is this God who invites us to speak?

> [The Lord says], "I was ready to be sought by those who did not ask for me;
>> I was ready to be found by those who did not seek me.
> I said, 'Here I am, here I am.'" (Isaiah 65:1)

> [Jesus said], "whoever comes to me I will never cast out." (John 6:37)

Jesus is close. He knows us better than we know ourselves, and he understands pain and suffering because he himself suffered. He certainly understands when life itself is threatened. If we think that our circumstances are beyond what Scripture identifies, perhaps we have forgotten that Jesus's pain and grief were so severe that he thought they would take his life before he could accomplish his mission (Mark 13:34). He is the right person for you. Your anxieties and fears remind you that you cannot control the smallest of details. To try to take charge, even of yourself, is beyond you. Right now, speak your anxieties to him instead of trying to solve them.

This is called faith. Faith simply acknowledges that you are desperate and needy, and only Jesus can give what you most deeply need. Your panic attacks have exposed the delusion that life is just fine—you can manage on your own—and it is good news when delusions are exposed. When we feel in control, we have no reason to turn to the Lord. We become numb to the source of life and joy, the most important relationship we can have. We approach the Lord as we would a wealthy but distant parent; we talk when we are short on cash. That's why Scripture warns against prosperity. During prosperity, we depend on ourselves and don't need help, or so we might think. Panic attacks break through that deception. You do, indeed, need help. That is the way you were created. This is the way of faith, and faith is one of God's great gifts to us. Faith means, "I need Jesus." That's why you talk to him. You need him, and he enjoys being needed. So speak those words to him. Say to him, "I need you."

As you find words to speak to the Lord, speak them with family and friends and be more public with your fears. Ask a few friends about their fears and anxieties, and what they do about them. If you have ideas on what help you need from God, ask someone to pray for you. You could pray that you will be more skilled in speaking to the Lord from your heart. You could pray that you will hear his good words to you.

A fine start. Now enter more fully into the gospel.

### "Remember the Gospel of Jesus Christ"

We know that Jesus died for our sins. That is the good news, or at least it is a critical part of it. Next, we bring this gospel to psychological problems. The apostle Paul wrote that, in this gospel, we find our true rescue and hope. "For I am not ashamed of the gospel, for it is the power of God for salvation to everyone who believes, to the Jew first and also to the Greek" (Romans 1:16).

Our task is to bring forgiveness of sins face-to-face with panic and discover how the knowledge of Jesus and what he has done are critical to our mental health.

Here is how a psalmist who was in great distress guides you.

> Out of the depths I cry to you, O Lord!
>     O Lord, hear my voice!
> Let your ears be attentive
>     to the voice of my pleas for mercy! (Psalm 130:1–2)

The psalmist cries out to the Lord, pleads with him to hear, and asks for help. He is *in extremis* and needs help immediately, or he could die. He invites you to join in and speak those words with him.

You might be surprised by what he says next.

> If you, O Lord, should mark iniquities,
>     O Lord, who could stand?
> But with you there is forgiveness,
>     that you may be feared. (Psalm 130:3–4)

The psalmist remembers the promise of forgiveness. That's his lifeline. These are his words of life when death is staking its claim. The insight is so powerful to him that the entire mood of the psalm changes from despair to confident waiting, rest, and even praise to God. This needs some explanation.

The psalmist is *not* suggesting that the cause of panic attacks is our sin. God knows we have valid and daily reasons for our anxieties. But our sin is the one thing that can separate us from God—not that he leaves us, but we turn from him, and such separation is *the* reason to be afraid. Sin has always been our most serious problem. But God, in Jesus Christ, forgives sin for the purpose of keeping us close to himself. "For Christ also suffered once for sins, the righteous for the unrighteous, *that he might bring us to God*" (1 Peter 3:18, emphasis added). The intent of the cross of Christ was to bring you close more than make you good. He, indeed, will produce good in you, but through forgiveness of sins, you are his, and he is yours.

When my grandchildren stay overnight at our home, the prized bedroom is right next to where my wife and I sleep. It feels safe. For those who are more prone to fear, that is not close enough. Only a late-night trip to our bed can calm them. Then, whatever might have been tormenting them is quieted. Our grandchildren don't exactly know what we could do to robbers, moving shadows, ghosts, and monsters, but they trust us and being close is enough for them.

All God's promises are fulfilled in *Immanuel*: God with us. This is the goal of forgiveness of sins. Scripture is the story of God's plan to be close to his people, and Jesus fully secured that closeness by his death and resurrection.

The apostle Paul puts it this way: "He who did not spare his own Son but gave him up for us all, how will he not also with him graciously give us all things? . . . For I am sure that neither death nor life, nor angels nor rulers, nor things present nor things to come, nor powers, nor height nor depth, nor anything else in all creation, will be able to separate us from the love of God in Christ Jesus our Lord" (Romans 8:32, 38–39).

The most profound way to be strengthened in the face of panic attacks is to confess sins and be certain of our forgiveness in Jesus, who bore the penalty of our sins. This is counterintuitive, especially given how our fears are natural to our vulnerable, human condition, and any talk about sin seems to miss the point, but it is worth trying. Though what we confess may be unrelated to anxiety and panic, confession is a regular feature of life with God. It assures us that Jesus, through the Spirit, is near.

You could confess how you love many things more than you love God, how you prefer that God keep his distance until you really need him, how you believe you are a pretty good person and God has reason to reward you for a life well-lived, or how you are a really bad person and God has reason to judge you harshly. Perhaps you are confident he could not love or forgive you, which suggests that you have to do better to earn his love and forgiveness, and that, of course, is a lie. Confess that you usually don't believe that the Father, Son, and Spirit love you. Then you remember that Jesus delights to forgive, and he says again, "whoever comes to me I will never cast out" (John 6:37b). In other words, end your confession with a simple "thank you."

As we practice this, the psalmist adds one more twist: "that you may be feared." Fear and closeness don't usually mix, but they do here. The psalmist uses fear in the sense that what we fear controls us. If we fear snakes, we are on high alert when we walk through a wooded glen. At that moment, we are blind to the beauty around us. Only snakes exist. If we fear germs, they dominate our thoughts, feelings, and actions. When we fear the Lord, we are controlled by both his love and power. He is close, and he is great. He is with us, and he is over all things. Love alone is not enough to push aside the objects of our fears. The fear of the Lord responds to his greatness or differentness. He is certainly not like us. The fear of the Lord is akin to awe.

From this secure place, panic attacks are a worthy occasion to take a hard look at your life. Though panic attacks often occur when you feel little or no anxiety, your body thinks differently. It senses threats and is ready to run. So a careful look can help. Here again, God's closeness makes all the difference. On your own, that examination might provoke more anxiety, which could provoke more attacks. So you muster the courage for your search by knowing that you are not alone. Jesus is your anchor and your rock. He holds you in the midst of storms.

Are there people walking with you? Are you listening to and learning from others? Perhaps you could talk about Psalm 130 with them. If you keep in step with the psalm, by the end you are talking to anyone who will listen about what God has done. Scripture teaches you how to walk with God, and that walk is best taken with a community.

Perhaps you could go further into your persistent anxieties. Have you been in dangerous situations? Have you ever spoken of these to the Lord? Have you ever felt under siege? What is threatened now? Are you running from failure? Do you sometimes feel as though so much depends on you, and you are not able to carry the load?

What are your doubts about God's words and God's love? These and other questions can be followed by speaking them to Jesus and considering how the gospel begins to speak hope into them.

The nearness of God, secured by the gospel, is a source of all kinds of comforts and wisdom. Here is a sample of other words God speaks to you as you are grounded in his forgiveness and remember his closeness.

1. *"You will be anxious."* *"When* I am afraid," writes the psalmist (Psalm 56:3a). In other words, you have good reasons to be anxious. Something important to you is at risk, and you are too small and weak to do anything about it. Your Father knows this, which means that he has compassion on you and he *will* act. Jesus calls us his "little flock" (Luke 12:32). He knows we are his defenseless lambs, and he assures us that he is our good shepherd.

   Yes, Jesus says, *"do not be anxious"* (Luke 12:22, emphasis added). But this is not so much a command as it is a promise of his presence. He uses the same language when he says to a woman who has experienced great loss, "Do not weep" (Luke 7:13). The words expressed his compassion and his assurance that he, indeed, would give her a reason not to weep. Notice the way we say similar words to children. "Don't worry, I'm here now." We are not commanding them to be fearless. We are asking them to listen to our words of comfort.

2. *"Give your attention to what is in front of you now."* Along with the promise of his presence, the Lord draws our

attention to today—not tomorrow but today. If you read about panic attacks, staying in the present is essential. Breathing exercises, for example, focus your scattered mind. They are a strategy to stay grounded now rather than take off into future fears. They are helpful, yet they are only a surface layer of help. God's words to you go deeper. They are embedded in the story of Israel's exodus from Egypt and God's provision of manna in the wilderness. He cared for them by giving them enough manna for only that day, and then he would do it again tomorrow. Today, he was saying, live with the manna, or the grace, he gives you. It is everything you need. Meanwhile, he is the one who will make the past right, he will "be anxious about tomorrow" (Matthew 6:34), and he gives you a mission right now that is enough to keep you busy. If that mission is unclear, look at what it is front of you. Is there work to be done? Rest to be taken? A person to love? If God's mission for you is unclear, ask others for help. In all this, God frees you to live in *today*.

3. "*Join faith to fear*." Soldiers will tell you that courage is not the absence of fear, but it is fear that still has duty in view. For you, this means that your anxieties will persist in some form, but they will also be attached to God's words—faith joined to fear—just like Psalm 56 and many other psalms. Faith reminds you of your duty, which is to trust him and express that trust in wisdom and love.

Then we can pray that our "little faith" grows. Jesus actually calls us "little faiths" (Matthew 6:30). Here again he is inviting us to know him even better, so we can grow up and have the faith of needy, dependent children. Adults, it turns out, are little faiths; children are big faiths. They hear the words of a parent and trust the parent. When the parent has made promises that they will be near and will stay vigilant during the night, a child can sleep. The plan is to have our large fears linked to an even larger confidence, trust, and rest. Our goal is to grow up and be a child.

## KEEP LEARNING, LISTENING, ASKING

From this safe home in Jesus, keep learning, listening, asking, growing, and inviting others to be part of it all with you. We were not intended to grow in Christ alone.

We can be reluctant to acknowledge our weakness and need for help. Men, especially, struggle to acknowledge their vulnerability and need. But if you have genuinely spoken of your neediness to the Lord, and you remember that the wise life is one of faith in Jesus rather than self-dependence, then you might be willing to ask others for help.

What makes this even more difficult is that psychological problems and psychiatric diagnoses have not lost their shameful associations. Most of us are willing to tell a friend that we had a doctor's appointment, but we don't want to say that we are seeing a counselor or a psychiatrist, and we certainly do not want anyone to know that we were in a psychiatric hospital.

Humility is a hard path, but it is the path of the wise. Humble, wise people seek help and advice. They track down reliable information, ask direction from friends and professionals, and read what they can. And through all of this, wise people ask for prayer.

Imagine something like these:

- "Could you pray this for me: 'God is our refuge and strength, a very present help in trouble' (Psalm 46:1). I need help."
- "I am filled with lots of fear. The one that is the hardest is that my daughter is not able to care for herself, and I fear for her when I die. Pray that Jesus will let me know his care for her, and pray for me that I will make wise decisions now for her future care."
- "Would you be willing to go for short walks with me? I am becoming more afraid to leave the house."
- "What has helped you when you have been afraid?"

What causes panic attacks? That is an irresistible question—one we *really* want to answer. But sometimes that best answer is, "I don't know." No one fully knows why anxiety, which is common to us all, is expressed in panic attacks only to some. This will *not* limit your ability to help or be helped. You do not have to know the exact causes of suffering—the eruption of physical symptoms in this case—to find help for that suffering. Trusting and coming close to Jesus helps more deeply than knowledge and insight.

As you continue that back-and-forth of hearing from those who have experience and bringing what you hear back to God, you will hear about medication, especially for panic attacks. We will consider medication when we get to depression. For now, approach medication with wisdom. Ask about its benefits and dangers. Medication will not address the deeper spiritual matters that are answered by God's presence and your trust in him, but it can quiet a body that feels under attack.

## QUESTIONS FOR REFLECTION

Since God's words always ask for a response, consider pausing and responding to a few questions.

1. What questions do you have? The better you understand, the more questions you have.

2. There are reasons we don't persist with the question, What does God say? One is that we simply don't think he has much to say. The topic is not in Scripture, so we look somewhere else. Are you seeing more of what God says? Is the treasure chest of his words to you filling up? What is the most helpful application of the gospel to your own anxieties?

3. Act today. What would be a wise, small step?

# Chapter 3

## TRAUMA

Even with only this brief example of how the Lord is over "every square inch" of anxiety and panic attacks, you can proceed with more confidence that Scripture does reach into your deepest struggles. Powerful and close, Jesus enters into the details of your life.

A diagnosis is about you and your body; psychotherapy is often about you, your body, and other people; God is about you and your body, other people, and him and . . . everything. "We impart a secret and hidden wisdom of God . . . . [T]hese things God has revealed to us through the Spirit. For the Spirit searches everything, even the depths of God. . . . Now we have received . . . the Spirit who is from God, that we might understand the things freely given us by God" (1 Corinthians 2:7a, 10, 12).

"The Spirit searches *everything*," and through Jesus Christ, we have the Spirit. How this transforms what we see in psychiatric diagnoses can be challenging, but we begin with confidence that God has spoken deeply in Scripture.

Let's turn to *trauma*. It has become one of the most common psychological words for past misery that follows us into the present. It can also contribute to panic attacks.

When you think of trauma you might first imagine an especially serious injury. Car accidents come to mind. Traumatic head injuries. Trauma centers. From its home in medicine, it has been applied to soldiers who are traumatized from seeing life-threatening and life-taking events. These traumas don't leave physical scars, but the pain and complex experiences last much longer than anything physical. It has become known as post-traumatic stress disorder (PTSD). The diagnosis now extends beyond the effects of war to many other brushes with death or evil—child abuse, domestic violence, rape, and sexual abuse. The diagnosis has been housed in secular psychotherapy. We want to bring it into Scripture and listen to what God says.

## LISTEN AND LEARN FROM OTHERS

Begin by finding words that describe your experience. This can be the most difficult feature of trauma. It leaves us with bodies that seem to have a mind of their own and minds that are restless, never settling into a promising course of action. So listen to what other people have said. What does trauma look and feel like? Here is one person's account.

Mary reacted to almost any noise or quick movement. Her friends came to expect her startle reflexes and joked about them. Not many understood that they were reflexes honed by years of abuse. Her husband understood, but it took years.

She lived with chronic anxiety marked by occasional panic attacks. When asked about her parents and family traditions, time stopped. Literally. She didn't move. She didn't respond. It was as if she was suddenly somewhere else. Later, she was able to describe pieces of her father's heavy drinking, his violence against her siblings, and, then, his sexual abuse of her.

Her childhood was isolated—she never entrusted herself to a friend. Her late teens and early twenties were marked by sexual encounters with men to whom she never said no. She wanted to stop them, but the words didn't come. She was frozen. At those times, she was never mentally present. Instead, she was blank and felt nothing. If she was unable to go blank, she made sure her imaginations were *not* in the present. But her lack of desire and numbness did not make her feel less guilty after these events. She felt guilt and shame after any sexual contact, and even more so when she followed Jesus during her late twenties.

At work and at church she could not say no. When her manager asked if she would consider an extra project, she did it. If you wanted something done, you asked Mary. And many people did. At this point, no one knew that Mary would be internally paralyzed by requests, as she was when people with power abused her as a child. (The word *dissociation* is used to describe this experience.) Rarely saying no, of course, brings challenges to a marriage. Her husband was generally patient, yet he often felt alone. He felt as if he never had the whole Mary.

The couple sought help from a pastor–counselor about her difficult work situation. One question led to another, and some of the past story came out over the course of a couple months. What was remarkable was that the reason she spoke was *not* because she trusted the pastor. She did trust him, but she needed something more persuasive if she were to speak openly. Shame, of course, demands to stay hidden. She spoke because she believed God himself asked her to speak. Her words were an expression of her faith in Jesus.

As the words came, the couple began to speak them in little bits, to the Lord. One small step, then another. She rarely could get the words out when she was alone and trying to pray. But she worked hard and began to look for more words. The following is a definition of PTSD that helped her to describe her experience:

- You have either experienced or witnessed a brush with death. The response was horror, helplessness, and intense fear.
- The past trauma intrudes into the present through memories, flashbacks, and nightmares. These intrusions can feel as though you are reliving the traumatic experience.
- You avoid reminders of the event—people, places, or anything that can trigger your memories.
- Your thoughts and moods seem to be without order. It is hard to remember important details of traumatic events, you make extreme interpretations about yourself and others, you always feel on high alert, blame gets confusing (e.g., you blame yourself when you were not the cause), you feel detached and distant from people and anything good.
- You can be reactive and irritable, prone to behaving recklessly and self-harm. You can have problems concentrating and sleeping.[3]

The couple also listened for words from other survivors. These came from friends, memoirs of abuse, and books such a Judith Herman's *Trauma and Recovery* and

Bessel van der Kolk's *The Body Keeps the Score: Brain, Mind, and Body in the Healing of Trauma*. These books help identify how the consequences of trauma can feel so physical. Victims "perceive their bodies as having turned against them."[4] They don't feel at home in the world, and they don't feel at home in their own bodies.

Chronic abuse, Herman observes, brings "surrender." With no way out, a survivor goes limp. That is as close to disappearing as you can get. Just say yes to anyone who is possibly stronger than you, then disappear. Here is the pathway to vivid, though disconnected, memories. Whereas most of us can tell a relatively coherent story of our lives, and we have a sense of who we are, trauma fractures events and leaves our sense of self in pieces, as if "flowing and spilling"[5] rather than solid and predictable. Everyday life can feel unreal. This sense of being detached from life and the feeling of *unreal* is why some trauma victims turn to self-injury. It feels real. No more detachment.

Van der Kolk reminds us that the body remembers the past, even if we ourselves only remember pieces. This is why Mary was startled at most anything. Her body was always on high alert. The body is not interested in a careful analysis about who is safe and who is dangerous, or who is good and who is bad. Better to assume that danger lurks everywhere, and no place is truly safe.

If you want to help, try to understand that Mary's reactions, given what she experienced, are normal. If death always seemed close, you would feel and act in similar ways. The better you know Mary, the more her world seems quite reasonable and is to be expected. As Mary realizes that she is not a freak, but is experiencing the well-known consequences of trauma, she learns to speak more freely.

## LISTEN TO GOD AND HIS PEOPLE

Now bring what you have learned back to God's house and hear what he says.

### "Speak to Me"

There is something about putting our past experiences into words that makes them more vivid and real. When we speak, we risk a torrent of memories as our past becomes more emboldened to enter the present. So words might emerge gradually. Speak what you can, if only, "Jesus, I need help."

Perhaps you will practice by speaking from your heart to a dear friend or counselor. Mary's story turned on the phrase "the couple sought help." But you might find that speaking to a friend and speaking to God are not tethered as much as you thought. Sometimes it will be much harder to talk to a person. More often, it will be harder to talk to God. Your friend, for example, was not a witness to the traumatic events, as was God. Your friend certainly could have done nothing about it. God, however, was there, and that complicates everything.

Say *something*. "I'm trying" might be one large step.

Psalms are always present in God's house. One way to use them is to listen until you hear words that express your truest feelings. Then you join in.

> Why, O Lord, do you stand far away?
>     Why do you hide yourself in times of trouble?
> In arrogance the wicked hotly pursue the poor.
> (Psalm 10:1–2a)

A fragment of a psalm is enough for now. Remember that these are words that God gives you to speak. He asks you, "Is it like this?" Other words will come as you discover that what Jesus did through the cross and resurrection are what your spirit needs most.

### "Remember the Gospel of Jesus Christ"

If you can't talk, try to listen. And what better place to start than by hearing about forgiveness? Our own sin does not cause trauma, but our daily sins can distance us from God. Every day we fail to love others well, and we certainly do not love God well. As sins accumulate, without confession and remembering his delight in us returning to him and being forgiven, we are more distanced and isolated. Forgiveness restores relationships and brings life. Hope exists because you are confident that he is with you.

If forgiveness of sins is ho-hum or seems like it is unable to pierce your mental or emotional pain, you are not yet seeing real life. In God's forgiveness you find inarguable evidence of God's love and faithfulness. When a woman showed extravagant love to him, Jesus made the observation that she loved him so much because she knew she was forgiven for so much (Luke 7:47–48). The principle still applies: when we know we have been forgiven for much, we know he loved much and we love him; when we are only forgiven for little, we love him little. It is in this mutual love—him for you and you for him—that life is most rich and free. The possibility for happiness and even joy rests here.

*The gospel proves that God loves you.* Forgiveness is love, and love affects everything. A man was going through his third of four chemotherapy treatments and barely had the energy to sip water. He survived. Ten years later when he recounts this era of great darkness in his life, he always talks about the neighbor who appeared in his backyard and cut his grass before it became unruly. He always cries when he remembers this act of love.

Love makes a difference, even when that love was only for a season, once every two weeks. It does not cure cancer or take away the present pain of past events, but it always makes a difference. It does not keep us from stumbling, but it cushions us from falls. "One will scarcely die for a righteous person—though perhaps for a good person one would dare even to die—but God shows his love for us in that while we were still sinners, Christ died for us" (Romans 5:7–8).

Or, as the apostle Paul wrote, Jesus "loved *me* and gave himself for *me*" (Galatians 2:20c, emphasis added). Paul went on to write that the way to know God's love is to pray to know his love. He even prays for us that we would "know the love of Christ that surpasses knowledge, that you may be filled with all the fullness of God" (Ephesians 3:19). Spiritual things are known by the Spirit giving them to us. Too often, if we do not know the love of Jesus for us, we have not asked.

*The gospel is that Jesus left heaven to find you, and he entered every dark place imaginable to do it.* The gospel is about being close to God. To do that, Jesus identified with you even to the point of entering into your afflictions. He determined that he would be weak in every way that you are weak and then be your suffering and crucified servant.

The book of Isaiah is filled with reports about Jesus, who came centuries later. After giving us hints of the child who would "be called Wonderful Counselor, Mighty God, Everlasting Father, Prince of Peace" (Isaiah 9:6c),

Isaiah settles into a section that begins with a servant. The servant is initially identified as Israel (41:8), and then the light falls on one servant alone (49:6). Jesus is the one who is disgraced, abandoned by all, and abused beyond recognition. When you read this, your mind is diverted from your own trauma and is riveted to his. You are familiar with suffering, so you see him vividly, as though he were up close, as though you were a witness. Then you are told that this is personal.

> He has borne our griefs
>   and carried our sorrows. . . .
> He was pierced for our transgressions;
>   he was crushed for our iniquities. (Isaiah
>   53:4–5)

You discover that his voluntary descent into this darkness was for you. The Servant served you by identifying with you and your pain, then, in some real way, he took that burden on himself so that you would not have to bear it. Instead, you take what is his, and he is now "high and lifted up" (52:13).

*The gospel proves that God knows you, and you can know him.* This, in itself, does not erase pain, but the *isolation* of pain can be as bad as the pain itself, and Jesus certainly breaks through that isolation.

Mary—the woman mentioned earlier who went through familial violence and sexual violation—can speak words to the Lord because, in love, he invites her to speak, and in love, he understands and responds with compassion and action. He knows her and her traumatic past because he too experienced them. Jesus is both her servant and her high priest. "For we do not have a high priest who is unable to sympathize with our weaknesses, but one who in every respect has been tempted as we are, yet without sin. Let us then with confidence draw near to the throne of grace, that we may receive mercy and find grace to help in time of need" (Hebrews 4:15–16). This is what you deeply desire.

My granddaughter endured her first wasp sting recently. I was affected by her pain for two reasons: I love her, and I have been stung by wasps and still remember the pain quite keenly. Pain sometimes wants *someone* who loves us and understands what we have been through, even without our having to explain it. Where this illustration breaks down is that I could do little about my granddaughter's pain. I could only wait with her until the pain subsided. But the compassion and sympathy of Jesus for you is a signal that *he* is doing something about it.

*The gospel of Jesus Christ cleanses you from shame.* Sometimes forgiveness, love, compassion, and empathy seem to fall short. You are forgiven through what Jesus did. There is no condemnation. That's certainly good news. You are loved. That, too, is good news. But then you walk out of the courtroom, free and declared righteous, and you feel just as disgusting as when you entered. A forgiven leper, loved and known, remains a leper. You still feel like hiding. The only possible solution, it seems, is to disappear, or not exist.

This is called shame, and you can find it in every culture and every church. Once I asked a group of respected religious leaders if they struggled with shame, and not just a struggle with a stray accusing thought but a struggle with near-debilitating, daily shame. Everyone raised a hand.

There is little comfort having comrades in shame. If you are a prisoner in solitary confinement, you find no solace in knowing that other prisoners are also isolated. Yet there might be a speck of good news in the sheer numbers. If so many people have a similar experience, and they made it through, then maybe there is a cure. If your doctor says, "Wow, I have never seen this before," you have reason to worry. But if she says, "Yes, I see this every day," then hope rises. And hope has good reason to rise. It just so happens that Scripture identifies shame as *the* human problem, and God specializes in compassion for its pain and promises for its cure.

Shame indicates that you are unpresentable because of something you have done or something done to you. It leaves you feeling worthless, cast off, and unclean, as though you could contaminate those around you. In Mary's case, shame was a result of sexual victimization, coupled with her sense that she was somehow responsible for what occurred.

The world around us certainly understands the deadly nature of shame. It tries to rebuild a semblance of self-esteem in a broken person. The problem with shame, however, is that the pollution of shame is quite real. It cannot be reasoned away or papered over by a more generous self-assessment. It must be removed. It must be cleansed. And the only way it can be removed is through the death of Jesus. Here is the story of how Jesus took our shame.

Hope rises when Jesus proclaims his mission statement.

The Spirit of the Lord is upon me,
  because he has anointed me
  to proclaim good news to the poor.
He has sent me to proclaim liberty to the captives
  and recovering of sight to the blind,
  to set at liberty those who are oppressed,
to proclaim the year of the Lord's favor. (Luke
4:18–19; also see Isaiah 61:1–2)

His people would be the excluded, outcasts, worthless, and those who never received favor. They were "tax collectors and sinners" (Matthew 9:11; 11:19), the demon possessed, the needy—people who were filled with shame. They included a Samaritan woman, to whom he revealed that he was the Messiah and with whom he had the longest recorded conversation in the New Testament. He treated her as a friend.

One story in particular reveals what was to happen at the cross. A woman had a discharge of blood. In that world, she was put to shame. She was unclean, an untouchable, not because of anything she had done but because of a disease. Her contamination was real. Blood and disease are associated with death, and a close association with death makes someone unclean. If you have suffered abuse, you too have known the contamination of death because death partners with Satan and evil perpetrators—together they attempt to separate people from Jesus. Contact with any of them means that you were unclean and needed God's cleansing. This unnamed woman was not allowed to touch other people, or they would be contaminated by her uncleanness. But she knew

Jesus better than most anyone of her day. She knew that he invited her to come close.

> She came up behind him and touched the fringe of his garment, and immediately her discharge of blood ceased. And Jesus said, "Who was it that touched me?" When all denied it, Peter said, "Master, the crowds surround you and are pressing in on you!" But Jesus said, "Someone touched me, for I perceive that power has gone out from me." And when the woman saw that she was not hidden, she came trembling, and falling down before him declared in the presence of all the people why she had touched him, and how she had been immediately healed. And he said to her, "Daughter, your faith has made you well; go in peace." (Luke 8:44–48)

Every detail reveals spiritual realities. She touched him. If you insert yourself in the story, *touch* is the same as *trust*. She saw him and touched him. You see him, so you trust him. That is faith. In that touch, Jesus took her shame. In exchange, he gave her power and holiness—which is a kind of cleanness that is permanent.

What happened to her shame? Jesus took her sin and shame, with all the abuse, rejection, and contempt that comes with them, and he put them to death. Shame was buried, powerless. In that death he brought down the reign of death, Satan, and all those who have acted on the evil one's behalf. He took away their power to separate people from God and others. He exiled these enemies and put *them* to shame by claiming his victory over them all, which is *your* victory over them. Shame is taken away by being associated with the right person—a person of great honor who binds himself to you in a way that you receive his honor, as you would when you marry a person of great wealth and that wealth becomes your own. That association with Jesus is sealed by simply saying, "Jesus, I need you."

Sometimes Scripture will identify the end of shame through Jesus's touch. Other times it comes from his face turned toward you in favor and love. "Those who look to him are radiant, and their faces shall never be ashamed" (Psalm 34:5). These are pictures of the gospel. Your life becomes tied to the life and death of Jesus. He takes all death, condemnation, and contamination on himself; you receive his life, righteousness, and holiness.

The apostle Paul writes about this union with Jesus in a simple way: you are "in him." Tucked away safely, protected by him, everything that is his is now also your own. This comes by faith. This faith does not shield us from the miseries of life, just as Jesus himself was not shielded from them. But union with Jesus has already broken the claims of death and shame, and that will be seen most clearly when he will make the whole world right.

*The gospel assures you of a future put right and made new.* The gospel is about the death and resurrection of Jesus, and it is that resurrection that assures us of a new direction in life. Stories depend on their ending. A person's cancer story turns on whether there is remission or recurrence. The intrigue and danger of Shakespeare's *Much Ado About Nothing* is lightened because the story ends well. Even an argument with a spouse feels different when the couple has a history of resolving arguments and emerging more unified than before. That is the gist of God's story with us. Injustice does not have the final word. The psalmist says, "I know that the LORD will maintain the cause of the afflicted, and will execute justice for the needy" (Psalm 140:12).

When you are *in Jesus*, your own story is no longer dominated by trauma or the perpetrators of abuse. Death will bring their ways to an end. Your own story, meanwhile, is told through the resurrection of Jesus and, as a result, brings assurance of resurrection and fullness of life.

The story of Job moves from great loss and proceeds to an end in which Job has so much more than he could have ever imagined. If you read the story closely, you know that the loss of children could not be overcome by the gain of many more children, but the story is trying to communicate that the beauty at the end, somehow, outweighs the pain that came before it. A betrayed spouse feels the sting of that betrayal until he can enter another relationship that is marked by faithfulness and love. The idea is that tears and fears will be wiped away.

The details include God's public judgment against all wrong (2 Timothy 4:1, 1 Peter 2:23), and our acting as wise judges along with him (1 Corinthians 6:2). Through it all, Jesus invites us to look and see. "Behold, I am making all things new" (Revelation 21:5). How this can take the pain of our pasts and leave them there, and then fill life with everything new, is less important than that it is happening and *will* happen.

### "Believe"

When you hear this good news, you listen, and then you respond. You do something. God's words are not mere education. They are more like marriage vows—he makes vows to you, and then it is your turn to respond. Your response might be, "Yes, Jesus, I believe." Change does not happen through information alone, no matter how pleasant that information might be. It emerges from trust or faith. "This is the work of God, that you believe in him whom he has sent" (John 6:29).

We are cleansed by faith (Acts 15:9), we "continue in the faith" (Acts 14:22), and we "live by faith" (Galatians 2:20). Faith can be expressed as "help," "thank you," "I believe you, and I believe *in* you," and "I need you." It is how people came under the protection of kings—"I am with you, and not with any other ruler." In that oath, a person's life was forever tied to the fortunes of that king. *Faith* means faith *in Jesus*, which means you abandon self-trust and independence and put all your trust in him.

Faith also means that you have not earned your relationship with him. In this sense, faith is contrasted with "works of the law" (Galatians 3:2), which suggests that your obedience brings his favor. Though we naturally believe that we have to perform in order to be loved, and that is the pattern of most human relationships, it is not true in Christ. He *is* love. You don't have to arouse it or hide less attractive parts of yourself to know his love to the fullest. He always loves first and most. The truth is that God has loved you while you were opposed to him. This is why neediness, desperation, and simply saying "help" are such important and simple expressions of faith. There is nothing else we can bring, and nothing else we are *asked* to bring.

Do you believe? Is your trust given to Jesus, crucified and risen? Or, as Jesus asked Peter, "Do you love me?"

(John 21:16). Jesus loved Peter first and most. Would Peter love Jesus in return?

Do you love him?

This is how life works in God's very personal kingdom.

- He loves you.
- You speak to him from your heart.
- He reveals himself most fully in the death and resurrection of Jesus.
- You put your faith in him, and, as you grow in faith, instead of becoming more self-sufficient, he only uncovers your need even more.

Having listened to God's good news, you respond, "I believe you." "Thank you."

Psalm 10 begins "Why, O LORD, do you stand far away?" After the psalmist pours out the details of what was done against him, and then remembers God's steadfast love, the psalm turns on a phrase, "But you do see" (v. 14), which means, "you see and you act on the victim's behalf." The psalmist ends with a declaration of his confidence.

O LORD, you hear the desire of the afflicted;
you will strengthen their heart; you will incline your ear
to do justice to the fatherless and the oppressed,
so that man who is of the earth may strike terror no more. (vv. 17–18)

Even if you can't say them yet, be encouraged; others have gone before you and have been able to speak these words. Someday you will say them too.

## KEEP LEARNING, LISTENING, ASKING, AND GROWING

PTSD, like the other struggles identified in this short book, does not go away, never to return. Instead, as soon as you think you might be done with it, you receive a surprise visit. This will be a reminder that you cannot make it through a day without speaking to and depending on Jesus.

All along the way you will be more open with other people. You will ask for prayer. You will tell more of your story. You will speak publicly about Jesus. You will be alert for good books, reliable information, and how others have been helped. Desperation is not proud. Whatever you read or hear, you hope to develop that rhythm of taking it back to your home in Jesus and watch how he reshapes and deepens everything.

One common observation is that the intrusive feelings and thoughts of PTSD can be so loud many affected people will look for ways to be distracted or numb themselves. Watch out for drugs and alcohol or other ways you try to self-rescue. Here is a rule that has no exceptions: when you look to be rescued by anything or anyone in this world, your rescuer will control you. Then your rescuer will become your master, and you will need to be rescued again.

Another common observation is that isolation is a danger sign. When you are increasingly silent, before God and other people, you will sink into darker and more hopeless places. The path of life is one that has more words and more people on it.

You will hear of two types of treatments for trauma, as well as for all psychiatric problems: medical and psychological. The medical treatments are usually medications that directly affect the body and brain. You will find that medications are not assumed to be of benefit for PTSD. They might, but they can also dull physical reactions in a way that you don't learn strategies to grow through them. The psychological therapies hope to indirectly alleviate physical symptoms, through yoga, meditation, and techniques to try to stay in the present and not be dragged off into the past. Psychological therapies also hope to talk about the past in such a way that it can remain there and not take over daily life. All these can lessen distressing symptoms, but they are not designed to reach into the soul.

You certainly hope to be able to tell your story. A friend or pastor is a natural place to do this. You will find that you learn more with each telling, especially if you keep returning to hear God's words to you. The first version will simply be an attempt to break through shame and be open. A later version will begin to include variations on words that God has said. "Behold, you God are against the shepherds [the perpetrators] (Ezekiel 34:10), you searched for me—your sheep (34:11), and you rescued me from their mouths (34:10)."

He has become our *good* shepherd, and in his judgment on the world, he will make all things right and new. Later, you can use Psalm 10 as a guide and use more and more of the word God invites you to speak.

Prayer will be the mainstay of help. When you pray, you can be sure that you are headed in the direction of life; you are in God's house. Let prayer be the final word of all your listening and asking and talking.

You pray, and you can ask for prayer. Imagine saying something like this: "I am struggling to apply the gospel to past experiences that still haunt me. Could you pray that I would have the gift of faith?" "I am afraid to say 'no' whenever I am asked almost anything. I want the discernment and courage to know when to say it. Could you pray as I know I will have to make those decisions this week?"

Such steps might seem small, but all good steps are small steps, and all growth and change follow this pattern. What might surprise you is not the slow, small steps, but that you can still feel quite weak and needy even as you grow. At those times, you can ask God to help you "behold" and see what he sees. Small steps are evidence of God's great power in you.

## QUESTIONS FOR REFLECTION

1. What questions do you have?

2. One of the most important skills we can learn is how to make connections between the gospel and the details of life. It certainly takes practice. Can you make that connection with a recent struggle in your life? As you reflect on this material on trauma, what connection was most meaningful?

3. Act today. What do you believe? What will you say to God and others?

# Chapter 4

# DEPRESSION

Next to be brought into God's house is depression. It is certainly common. Either you or someone you love has experienced it. Because you are probably familiar with it, let's first listen to God. With trauma, we began by listening to those with experience because the descriptions of trauma's aftershocks are not detailed in Scripture and we wanted to find words. This time we will begin with God's words and the words of his people. Then we can listen to what those around us are saying. Medication, of course, is on our agenda.

## LISTEN TO GOD AND HIS PEOPLE

Start by remembering how God's care is not like our own. If you have been depressed, people in the church have said words that hurt. Many of us have been clumsy in our care for depressed souls, and God's compassion takes a stand on their behalf. We are short on understanding and empathy. We think we understand because we once had a bad day and felt "depressed," but we snapped out of it the next day. Other people should snap out of it too. "Just be thankful," we might say, though any sentence that begins with *just* is simplistic, inaccurate, and hurtful. "Shouldn't Christians always feel a little better than good?" Depressed people have valid reasons not to feel at home in a church.

So you remember that God is compassionate. He is moved by your pain. On his heart, therefore, is how those who struggle with depression have been misunderstood and mistreated even by people in his house. You forgive those who have been zealous and wrong in their advice, who have spoken without listening, who have listened but without grief. Then, armed with God's patience, you head out to find someone who might understand. You ask them to be patient with *you*. The more severe the pain, the more important it is to include others. Look for those you know to be wise and caring.

You could tell the story of depression in your life. You could ask them to pray that you would be able to speak from your heart to the Lord.

*God asks, "Is this how you feel?"* C. H. Spurgeon is one of the better-known Christians who has written about his own depression. He said, "You may be surrounded with all the comforts of life, and yet be in wretchedness more gloomy than death if the spirits be depressed. You may have no outward cause whatever for sorrow, and yet in the mind be dejected, the brightest sunshine will not relieve your gloom."[6]

As the descriptions pile up, you hear recurring images. Death, emptiness, darkness, unbearable pain, worthlessness. Misery that is immovable. Haunting fears. Depression that appears for no apparent reason. Muted colors. The world becomes shades of black and white. Some days depression can be less oppressive, other days intolerable. At its worst, even if your circumstances are peaceful and prosperous, you feel as though everything good has suddenly been removed from life and has been replaced by nothing.

Words will be hard to find. Our language is fuller and more descriptive during euphoria than it is in dysphoria. So you might borrow some words: "My God, my God, why have you forsaken me?" (Psalm 22:1). These are the words of Jesus, who is the person behind all the psalms. Jesus himself "cried out with a loud voice, saying, 'Eli, Eli, lema sabachthani?' that is, 'My God, my God, why have you forsaken me?'" (Matthew 27:46). His grief alone brought him close to death. He invites you to say these words with him.

The apostle Paul follows this tradition. He said, "We do not want you to be unaware, brothers, of the affliction we experienced in Asia. For we were so utterly burdened beyond our strength that we despaired of life itself" (2 Corinthians 1:8).

Do Paul's words describe what you experience?

When you search the psalms for more words, you discover verses in Psalm 88.

> For my soul is full of troubles . . . . (v. 3a)
> I am a man who has no strength,
> like one set loose among the dead . . . . (vv. 4b–5a)
> You have put me in the depths of the pit . . . . (v. 6a)
> Your wrath lies heavy upon me,
> and you overwhelm me with all your waves. (v. 7)
> Darkness is my closest friend. (v. 18 NIV)

That's what depression feels like.

For those who want to help, two things come to mind. First, this can be overwhelming trouble. Allow your compassion to be aroused. We want the suffering of a depressed person to move us. Second, we wonder why. Why is our friend depressed? This is a question with no clear answer, and we should be careful with it. Job's friends felt compelled to find the reason for Job's misery, and they were wrong. Those who knew the man born blind wanted to know the cause of his blindness. They reasoned that the cause was either the blind man's sin or his parent's sin (John 9:1–3). It wasn't. We have a history of getting it wrong. So we don't jump to conclusions about why. We certainly don't conclude that depression is the result of our friend's sin. Humility should lead us to say, "I don't know why you are going through this."

But aren't we supposed to praise the Lord continually? Indeed, when we know Jesus, who is the reason for joy, our suffering is buffered by hope. But a quick read of Scripture reveals that suffering is everywhere and weakness is to be expected. God does not promise health and prosperity in this world. That lie should have been put to rest when Jesus went through the worst of suffering and pain. What he promises is that he will be with us in our sufferings. What we expect is that there will be times we weep, and there will be times when weeping might be interrupted by moments of rest.

God's Word reminds us that we will be "burdened beyond our strength." We will feel desperate. Paul himself couldn't understand this at first. He expected that life in Christ would feel strong, healthy, and protected from the worst of suffering. But then, after his third time praying to be relieved of his "thorn" (2 Corinthians 12:7), he realized that God's power was best on display in his weakness because then he had no choice but to depend on him. This is how weakness became the new normal in the Christian life. Think of words such as *persevere*, *endure*, *wait*, and *hope*. They assume that afflictions can stay with us.

The complexities pile up. There is so much we do not understand, but in God's house, there is a simplicity to his care. First, we invite the person to speak about the pain of depression, and our compassion is aroused. While depression leans toward what's-the-use and prefers silence, we invite words. Once we find a handful of words or images that describe depression, we will find dozens more. The more difficult part is to speak those words to the Lord.

### "Speak to Me"

Depression is a lead-cased room. Nothing good is allowed in, and nothing within you reaches the world outside. Words spoken fall to the floor as though they were absorbed into the bottomless pit itself. Everything you experience assures you that you are right to be hopeless. All this makes actual words spoken to Jesus seem impossible.

A few questions might help: Do you believe that the one who made the ear will hear? Do you believe that he hears *you*? Remember that he hears us because that is who he is. "The hearing ear and the seeing eye, the Lord has made them both" (Proverbs 20:12). He hears everyone who calls to him. Though speaking to him might seem meaningless, if he asks you to speak, he has good reasons, and those reasons are for your benefit.

Say *something*. Say *something*.

### "Remember the Gospel of Jesus Christ"

With a mind that feels emptied of all things good, it will help to remember the gospel. Only the gospel invitation can equip us to call out to God when we face such a formidable darkness.

*The gospel is about Jesus, who did what you could not do.* I have heard faithful helpers say to their depressed friends, "I will believe for you, when you can't," "I will pray for you, when you can't," "I will hope for you, when you can't." And Jesus is that faithful helper and friend.

This help began in earnest when he was led into a lifeless wilderness, without food for forty days, and was tempted by Satan. He did this because we wither in the face of deep trouble and temptations. When impossible moments arise, we turn to our own wits or alcohol or despair, so Jesus turned to the Father *for us*, on our behalf. His response to Satan's temptations came from the book of Deuteronomy: "man does not live by bread alone, but man lives by every word that comes from the mouth of the LORD" (Deuteronomy 8:3; also see Matthew 4:4). He said this for you.

Jesus lived for us with wholehearted dependence on his Father. We are unable to do that without his help. He is your champion and your perfect representative to the Father. His obedience is attributed to you, as you rest in Jesus alone. King David illustrated this when he represented Israel against the giant Goliath. His obedience to God and his victory were dispersed to all the people, as though they themselves had fought.

For us, where we were weak, Jesus believed his Father's words and obeyed. He did this to bring you to God. In the weakness of depression, there are times when you hear misery and death more loudly than the words of God's love for you. At those times, your hope is that someone else believed those words on your behalf. He was your King David. You can rest in his obedience and victory, which, after all, is your primary, spiritual job. "Come to me, all who labor and are heavy laden, and I will give you rest. Take my yoke upon you, and learn from me, for I am gentle and lowly in heart, and you will find rest for your souls. For my yoke is easy, and my burden is light" (Matthew 11:28–30).

Now press into your response. Do you hear what Jesus said to you? Do you have a reason to push his words aside? There is no other place where you will find life. What do you need to be able to hear? Do you believe what he says? Do you love him?

When the gospel is offered to you, you must do something, even if it is, "Yes, I believe. Help my unbelief."

*The gospel is about Jesus, who is praying for you.* Jesus obeyed where we did not, and now he prays for us when our words seem to fail. "Christ Jesus is the one who died—more than that, who was raised—who is at the right hand of God, who indeed is interceding for us" (Romans 8:34). The Spirit, who Jesus sent to dwell with you and in you, also prays for you. "The Spirit helps us in our weakness. For we do not know what to pray for as we ought, but the Spirit himself intercedes for us with groanings too deep for words" (Romans 8:26).

Heaven is quite busy when depression renders you powerless.

- The Spirit knows what is most deep in your heart, and he brings those depths to the Father when you can't.

- Jesus prays for you. All heaven hears from him that you are not condemned because of what he has done in forgiving your sins once and for all.
- The Father is delighted to hear and show mercy. The reason the divine plan included the prayers of the Son and Spirit on your behalf is *not* that the Father is reluctant to show mercy. The reason is to give prominence to the Son and the Spirit and have prayer come to him in the name of Jesus.

Jesus prayed for you (John 17:20–24), and he prays for you now. Your life belongs to him because you trusted Jesus to do what you could not. You could not purchase a suitable sacrifice for your sins; you could not earn God's favor by being unusually good. You *can* understand that you are spiritually powerless in yourself, and you can ask for his mercy to you in Jesus. You can rest. He will pray for what you need most.

*The gospel unites you to Jesus, and you can pray his prayers.* Your prayers to the Lord do not make you more acceptable or holy, but they do bring more life to your soul. As you are able, you try to say something to him. The easiest way to do this is by joining Jesus in his prayers. As our true king and representative, he is the true psalmist.

Among the words Jesus prayed were, "How long?"

How long, O Lord? Will you forget me forever?
　　How long will you hide your face from me?
How long must I take counsel in my soul
　　and have sorrow in my heart all the day?
How long shall my enemy be exalted over me?
(Psalm 13:1–2)

He also prayed with more obvious desperation: "My God, why have you forsaken me?" (Psalm 22:1). He prayed them so you can pray them. If you can force them out of your mouth, you are watching God's strength in your weakness. You are watching the Spirit at work in you. You are turning to God even when he *feels* far away and you feel like you are nothing. *That* is spiritual strength.

Now go back to Psalm 88 and find more of Jesus's words.

> For my soul is full of troubles, and my life draws near to Sheol [the grave]. (v. 3)

> O LORD, why do you cast my soul away?
>   Why do you hide your face from me?
> Afflicted and close to death from my youth up,
>   I suffer your terrors; I am helpless. (vv. 14–15)

Once you speak those first words *to* Jesus and *with* Jesus, the words might come easier, as though you opened a conduit to your soul. Then you can try some of the other words in his psalms. Among the most challenging will be the introduction to Psalm 88. It begins, "O LORD, God of my salvation, I cry out day and night before you" (v. 1). Jesus is talking to his Father. When he feels himself sinking, he says it again, "I, O LORD, cry to you; in the morning my prayer comes before you" (v. 13).

You see why the words are challenging. Jesus leads you to confess that his Father and your Father hears, and you can come to him again and again, with confidence. You don't necessarily share Jesus's confidence, but with what little faith you have, you can say the words with him.

When my wife and I read books to our children, their favorite books usually had a familiar refrain or cadence. They listened and enjoyed them. But as we kept reading those books, the tradition changed. Once we came to the especially familiar parts, our girls spoke the words with us. It was a double delight. They delighted in "reading" the book; we delighted in the shared words. And every once in a while, we laughed together when we broke into a scary rendition of "the big hungry BEAR."

We share something intimate with Jesus when we speak his words with him, and he delights in it.

Will this take away your depression? No. In this world, you will have trouble, but as you persevere in faith and maturity, you may notice that depression is wrapped in hope, purpose, and reasons to live. It might feel lighter. But you will also notice that depression seems to have a mind of its own. Some hours it might feel less heavy; some seasons it may leave. There are many things we do not understand.

## LISTEN AND LEARN FROM RELIABLE SOURCES

So we return to the question about what causes depression. Scripture leaves the options open: terrible life circumstances that take a physical toll, biological changes in the brain, or matters of the heart such as anger, guilt, and shame that begin to affect the body. In other words, given persistence and time, different paths could end in depression—both spirit and body can play a role.

Given the uncertainties about the cause of depression, we expect that help may cast a wide net. It considers physical treatments that could lighten symptoms. It is an occasion to face past hardships or fears that still exert their power. It pauses on any present troubles, such as disrupted relationships, guilt, anger, and fear. These are not necessarily the cause of depression, but they are certainly important as you bring every square inch to Jesus. Through all this, depression is always a time to examine your reasons for hope. Hopelessness runs through all depression. When you ask for help, be sure to ask others to read Scripture about hope until you hear one verse that gets through the darkness. This is, in part, how Scripture approaches the question of causes and treatments.

Given the possible causes, especially the possible physical causes, we listen and ask others who have experience. Long before the rise of modern psychiatry and psychotherapy, many thoughtful people assumed that depression or melancholia was tied to something physical. When you listen to depression, you hear of experiences that are *at least* physical. Fatigue, changes in appetite, the simultaneous experience of both pain and the absence of feeling, thinking that feels slowed and ineffective. Spurgeon believed there was a physical origin for his own depression, as did Martin Luther for his. For them, this meant that they both clung to Jesus and considered ways to quiet the physical symptoms.

Medical research does not diminish the value of counseling or even talking with a trusted and wise friend, but it emphasizes medication, and it assumes that a chemical imbalance is a prominent cause. Medication, it turns out, is not *the* answer that it was once hoped to be. If it were, there wouldn't be the proliferation of talk therapies and a growing list of proposed physical treatments. The search for one cause remains a mystery, and depression likely has multiple causes. While that search continues, medication will be the most commonly prescribed treatment.

Medication tends to be prescribed *as needed* for panic attacks, and there is no definitive medication protocol for trauma. With depression, however, it is often a first-line defense. So in discussing depression, it makes sense to take a closer look at medication and physical treatments.

Our goal is to bring research observations into God's home in which he speaks to every square inch of his creation. What does God say about the body and its treatment? To answer this, we still want to maintain our links to the gospel.

## BACK TO GOD'S HOUSE AND HIS WORDS

The gospel is about the body, its weakness and its resurrection. The realm of the spiritual is not limited to the unseen. Whatever his spirit animates and renews is spiritual, and that spiritual work certainly extends to our bodies. Our bodies are essential to who we are and why Jesus died. His death was a bodily death, and he was resurrected to a "spiritual body." Today, our bodies are weak, fragile, and wasting away, and our strength is in his word to us and his Spirit making them alive. Someday, our bodies will be new.

> For [Jesus] was crucified in weakness, but lives by the power of God. For we also are weak in him, but in dealing with you we will live with him by the power of God. (2 Corinthians 13:4)

> Christ has been raised from the dead, the first-fruits of those who have fallen asleep. For as

by a man came death, by a man has come also
the resurrection of the dead. For as in Adam
all die, so also in Christ shall all be made alive.
(1 Corinthians 15:20–22)

Scripture describes us as embodied souls—we are
both physical and spiritual. We could say we are hybrids,
both from earth and heaven. These two building blocks
are miraculously fused. They belong together, but the dis-
tinction makes sense. For example, we naturally describe
ourselves as more than our bodies. An amputation takes
away something we possess—"my foot"—but we ourselves, somehow, remain the same.

Our body, which includes our brain, is the material building block of our humanity. It is identified as
strong or weak. When it is strong and works well, we are
rarely aware of our physical being. When it is weak and
unhealthy, the body draws attention to itself and looks
for relief. Bodily weakness includes fatigue, pain, heart
failure, and muscular weakness. When the weakness is
related to the brain, the symptoms can be more complicated: memory problems, dyslexia, proneness to distrac-
tion, hallucinations, confusion, and depression.

Sometimes these brain-related symptoms can be
mistaken as sinful disobedience. For example, when a
dementing adult begins to forget his children's names, the
children can take that as a lack of love, at least initially.
But the body does not have the ability to make us sin or
make us obey God. Scripture never calls our bodies right
or wrong. What they can do is put limits and restrictions
on our hearts' intents. For example, we might want to
reach out and encourage a friend, but sickness or brain

disorders limit some expressions of love. We might aspire to be mathematicians or mechanics, but our brains and bodies are unable to perform at the levels necessary. We might prefer to be able to do more than drag ourselves out of bed, but the brain and body have other plans.

Our soul (or spirit, mind, inner person, heart) sets the spiritual and moral course of life. In our hearts or souls, we know God and live before him. Decisions between right and wrong are within its jurisdiction. Faith or trust—dependence on Jesus Christ—is its highest calling.

The body can be strengthened, and it can be weak; the soul can grow in faith in Jesus even during those weaknesses. Here are two passages that illustrate those differences.

> While bodily training is of some value, godliness is of value in every way, as it holds promise for the present life and also for the life to come. (1 Timothy 4:8)

> We do not lose heart. Though our outer self [the body] is wasting away, our inner self is being renewed day by day. For this light momentary affliction is preparing for us an eternal weight of glory beyond all comparison, as we look not to the things that are seen but to the things that are unseen. For the things that are seen are transient, but the things that are unseen are eternal. (2 Corinthians 4:16–18)

These point to a few guiding principles.

1. Our body, our "outer self," can be afflicted in many ways, psychiatric diagnoses among them.

2. Physical treatments are of "some value." They can change the physical symptoms of a body: they can decrease pain, quiet a disordered mind, reduce fatigue, and lessen the pain of depression. That body will, however, eventually waste away and be raised a "spiritual body" (1 Corinthians 15:44) that will never know weakness or decay. Spiritual training—knowing, trusting, and following Jesus—has "value in every way." In contrast to physical treatments that might be of benefit only on this side of death, spiritual training has enduring benefits that extend even beyond death.

Here Scripture brings medication into its long reach. Medication does not raise a moral question: Is it right or wrong to take medication? The question is, Is medication beneficial? Might it strengthen us? To answer those questions, we turn to those who have seen the effects of medications or experienced those effects. Then we make a decision. Sometimes the medication will help; sometimes it won't. Either way, you have freedom to make wise decisions about medicine and other physical treatments. If medication can quiet a body that seems turned against you, that is good, assuming that the physical costs of those treatments do not outweigh the benefits.

Scripture adds this: physical treatments might have important benefits; spiritual growth in the midst of troubles has even more lasting and deeper benefits. We could say for *any* medical treatments that we do not put our deepest hope in them, just as we do not put our full hope in anything that we can see, such as a spouse, children, a job, or a bank account. We hope in Jesus who, by his Spirit, strengthens our souls during our troubles. This means that when we take medication it is an occasion to redouble our efforts in knowing Jesus, searching for his comfort and wisdom, enjoying forgiveness of sin, and remembering our calling to love others.

Notice how this approach clarifies how God speaks to every square inch of life. It does not mean that there is a list of psychoactive drugs in the Old Testament, with their dosage levels and specific uses. God's words to us include his call to look, listen, study the body and brain, and use that knowledge wisely. We ask other people for help.

What God's words *do* is let us see more. For example, we all see quartz, granite, diamonds, and coal as different types of rock. They are God's rocks, and he invites us to study and use them. But only God can reveal that, seen correctly, rocks speak of God as our enduring, unchangeable, unshakable foundation. Each rock reflects the Creator and, in a pinch, could be called upon to give him praise.

In a similar way, we also see people: cell structure, personality, even ironies in which beauty and degradation exists in the same person. But God's words reveal so much more. Because God values people more than rocks and people are like him in every way a creature could be like the Creator, he says so much more. We see human purpose, the beauty of love, the impossibility of the independent life, and how everything we truly want is found in Jesus Christ and his gospel. When God opens our eyes, it is as if we once saw in two dimensions and now we see in three.

As we listen to the world around us, antidepressant medication will be what we hear most often. Dig a little more, however, and we will discover no end to physical treatments alleged to have some value. Light therapy, changes in diet, allergies, endocrine imbalances, and exercise are among them. Nonmedical interventions also proliferate. Most of them are ways of dealing with unhelpful thoughts, pursuing good relationships and avoiding bad ones, and learning how to live today. All of these could have some benefit. Yet real explanations remain hard to find. The brain both affects how we live, and it is affected by how we live. It affects how we experience all of life, and it is chemically changed by trauma, intense fear, guilt, shame, love, faith, and hope. Careful examination of possible causes is a complex process.

Meanwhile, Scripture speaks of a deeper healing of our souls that comes through joining with him by a simple response of faith or trust. Humans cannot truly thrive unless we hear and take to heart what God says about us, our purpose and our need.

## QUESTIONS FOR REFLECTION

1. What questions do you have?

2. Make the connection between the gospel and a recent struggle in your life. As you reflect on this material on depression, what connection is most meaningful?

3. How are you growing in the way you speak to the Lord about matters that are on your heart? Now would be a fine time to keep at it.

# Chapter 5

# NARCISSISM

Narcissism is a different type of disorder. As you learn about it, you find that the narcissist's past gives few helpful clues, and the research is relatively silent about medication and physical causes. But like other psychological descriptions, once you notice it, you see it everywhere, and there seems to be more of it. It is an important human experience to which we ask, What does God say?

The story of Narcissus comes from Greek mythology and was later popularized by Sigmund Freud in his monograph, *On Narcissism: An Introduction*. It is now a word we hear often and a label that is regularly applied (always to others, not to ourselves). The myth is about the handsome Narcissus who rejected the affection of Echo and was punished by the gods for causing her pain. The punishment was he would fall in love with his own reflection, which he did when he saw his face reflected in a pool of water. He never left that reflection and died there. This means that the basic idea of narcissism is to blatantly care about oneself above all others. All adoration and attention must be directed to that person. Other people are a mirror that reflects the narcissist's beauty and greatness. As a result, narcissists seem to be unable to have meaningful, mutual relationships, and they don't seem to care.

This introduces quite a different starting point for you. The narcissist has no problem, at least none that he or she feels. If there is any problem, it is you. Your disloyalty, your base ignorance and overt stupidity, your lessness. So you begin by finding words that help you understand someone else. You first go out and listen to what others are saying.

## LISTEN AND LEARN FROM OTHERS

Narcissism has been called narcissistic personality disorder. A personality disorder simply means a stubbornly enduring and pervasive pattern is in someone's life. Other diagnoses are described as something you have and prefer to be rid of, but personality disorders identify characteristic features of a person.

The basic definition from *DSM–5* includes

- grandiose sense of self-importance;
- fantasies of unlimited success, power, beauty, and so on;
- pervasive sense of being special;
- requires admiration;
- sense of entitlement;
- exploits others;
- lack of empathy;
- envious of others, and believes that others envy him or her;
- arrogant and haughty.[7]

In other words, it is always their birthday. Today, tomorrow, and the next day are dedicated to their interests and desires, so don't expect that you will be known or understood. Your purpose is to be a mirror that reflects their perceived image of themselves. You are the admiring audience; they are special.

No empathy here. No room for guilt either. If you interfere with the party, expect to receive their anger. That anger might come at you as a bully who wants power and control or as one who doesn't even have time for you, so they turn away. Expect lasting grudges. They have plenty of rules for you, but the rules don't apply to themselves. Greed and power are their go-to moral principles.

You will also notice that they are hypercompetitive. They have to win, but they don't want competition. Losing is their version of horror and shame. Control and power protect them from losing and humiliation, and they *will not* be humiliated, though they seem vulnerable to a mere slight.

Faithfulness in marriage is not their strong suit. Children are a possession. As their children grow, some of them will always try to win the temporary favor of the narcissist. Others will give up and turn away from the relationship.

Though these behaviors are blatant, they might not be immediately troublesome for a casual observer. Narcissists can have an initial charm—it works to their advantage—and their immunity to consequences can make them appear bold and daring. They might say what you wish you could say. And isn't it nice to occasionally be with the person who is the life of the party? But most everyone, over time, has the eerie sense that the narcissistic person is hollow. There is little substance. Nothing is below the surface.

This description overlaps with those for antisocial personality and borderline personality. (Antisocial personality disorder is the larger category for terms such as *sociopath* or *psychopath*.) The antisocial personality might not be on a quest for admiration but, along with the narcissist, shares a lack of empathy and relational feelings, a lack of insight into self and others, and being unaffected by consequences, all with a superficial charm.

Could they be described as hollow? In one sense, yes. Inner substance usually consists of passion, pain, desire, aspirations, attachments to people, and self-awareness. You will have to search hard for any of these from a narcissist. But you will discover that the person has his or her logic. You might be amazed by how people simply don't figure into that logic—that is, love does not figure into it—but there is, at least, a thought process. In contrast to the narcissist, mischief created by the antisocial personality is calculated but impersonal, as if they are on a quest to find ways to repel boredom more than to satisfy an insatiable ego.

Borderline personality disorder shares a common core of a self-focus and lack of insight with narcissists and antisocial personality. They make judgments about other people that are often inaccurate and immune to correction. They also appear hollow and empty, in their own way. What distinguishes them is the intensity of their feelings. Like narcissists, they are always scanning for rejection and searching for a person who can perfectly meet their needs for being understood and affirmed. You will notice them when they value you among all others. You alone have been a good friend, whereas everyone else has deeply wounded them. You alone have truly listened to them and understood them. But expect to have your allegiances tested. Will you be there for a late-night phone call? Will you leave your schedule open for when you are needed most? In other words, you will soon be cut off when you don't fill their inner emptiness, which can never be filled. Perhaps, if you show the appropriate grief for your perceived offenses, and you do the suitable penance, you will be reinstated, only to fall short again.

There are commonalities in these descriptions, but in what follows, I will especially have the narcissist in mind.

## LISTEN TO GOD

Scripture seems to identify the narcissist easily. Here is the prototype of sin. Haughty, lover of self (2 Timothy 3:2), and spiritually dead. End of story. Case closed. The cause of a narcissist's maddening lifestyle. Confession and God's forgiveness are the answer. But for a number of reasons, this can't be the end of what God says. One reason is it doesn't explain enough. We are all sinners and can say with the apostle Paul, "Wretched man that I am!" (Romans 7:24), but we are not all narcissists. A second reason is these judgments must be surrounded by self-judgments, and we will start there.

As a way to curb our own frustration with narcissists, note the similarities we share with them. "Woe to you, scribes and Pharisees, hypocrites! For you clean the outside of the cup and the plate, but inside they are full of greed and self-indulgence" (Matthew 23:25). We are the Pharisees. The seeds of narcissism are in us all, and this, of course, is a critical starting point.

We are all familiar with our overflowing self-concern and desire for the attention and regard of others. This insight will help. But there remains the eerie sense that this person is also different from you. Hollow, unable to look in a mirror and see an accurate picture of themselves. They are shameless. Humanity is a composite of sin and remnants of the character of God that is dispersed among us all. In the worst of people, we can usually find something good. But here, the good is barely perceptible.

*The gospel is for embodied souls.* When we get to the brink of losing all patience, certain that the narcissist is simply mean and self-centered, we consider how Scripture provides more than one way to understand other people. We are souls who can sometimes seem spiritually dead. We are also embodied, and the body imposes strengths and weaknesses.

## DETAILS ABOUT THE BODY AND BRAIN

Everyone can acknowledge that we are a collage of strengths and weaknesses, but we add a fatal attachment to this reality. When it comes to judging others, we assume that people are like us, with our assorted strengths and weaknesses. If we are able to resist a shot of whiskey, the alcoholic should too. If we can show respect to others, then other people should be able to do the same. But other people do not share our strengths and weaknesses. When it comes to taking a hard look at ourselves, pride can make us see only someone else's problems. But self-examination is also an ability—a strength or weakness. Some of us do this easily and accurately; some of us don't know what it means or how to do it. After a brain injury, for example, what is most frustrating to family members is that brain-injured people do not understand their own disabilities and are prone to endlessly making the same mistakes. Sadly, we can mistake that inability as being hopelessly self-centered.

Here is a general rule: the more physical and brain weaknesses we see in another person, the more patient we become, and with patience comes wiser and potentially more helpful words. As a result, we try to understand the abilities of a narcissist.

*Emotion-less.* A self-described sociopath, kin to narcissists, observed, "I feel like my risk-seeking behavior stems from a low fear response or a lack of natural anxiety in potentially dangerous, traumatic, or stressful situations."[8] In other words, this person doesn't feel fear or anxiety like the rest of us. Without those feelings telling us, "You will be sorry if you do that," expect recklessness and risks that carry a high probability of failure.

Dulled emotions can also affect our view of the future. One feature of narcissists is that their lives are trapped in the present. They are poor at anticipating future difficulties and rarely make plans. Arrogance, of course, doesn't listen to any advice, but add to that arrogance an inability to feel consequences, and there is no reason to prepare for future problems because future crises simply don't *feel* like problems. Perhaps those problems, when they come, make the person feel *something*, which he or she welcomes.

If a narcissist doesn't feel as much as others, imagine how this will affect empathy. Empathy is an expression of love. It means that you can understand, at least in part, the feelings of others, and you are affected by both how they feel and the events that provoked those feelings.

Such empathy is a spiritual matter, yet it depends on certain abilities that rely on the brain.

Our brains regulate and provide the neurological base for our emotional range. Some of us are exuberant and hopeful. Some are darker, brooding. Others are emotionally steady and less affected by the events around them. Some experience shades of frustration and little else. These differences have their reasons, and the brain is one of them.

There is a direct link between your own emotional experience and empathy. If you feel intensely, you will be more capable of feeling intensely on behalf of others. If you feel rejection, you will understand others who feel rejection. If you *don't* feel rejection, you won't be sympathetic when those you love are rejected. If you *don't* register fear or danger as much as others, you will not have sympathy for them in their fears. If you do not have certain feelings because your brain has a limited emotional range or because you have learned to deny those feelings, you will be handicapped in your compassion.

If these observations actually fit, they will affect the way you relate to a narcissistic person. For example, you will be less offended by their apparent indifference to you—it is not necessarily personal. You will also be less prone to expecting your emotional tone—your hurt, your anger—to have any impact. Narcissists can be confused by empathy or requests for it. Instead of judging them as amoral through and through, you might approach them as those who come from a different country and speak a different language, and you have to figure out how to have basic communication with them. From this perspective, you might find that the person is actually trying to have a relationship more than you thought.

Now add the possibility of a disability in making assessments of personal strengths and weaknesses. Some of us are fairly accurate in those assessments, some of us see weaknesses and no strengths, and others see all strengths and no weaknesses. Those who fit the descriptions of narcissist seem to be poor at assessing their weaknesses. They are all strengths, no weaknesses. This might be another reason to ignore the future. When people believe they can master anything, they will bring this mastery to any future problems. This can be catastrophic for families, and the narcissist will be unsympathetic because it will not feel catastrophic for him.

Why won't they just listen to you and your feedback on them? If you have a friend who suggests you are not as good at math as you thought, you might listen; you might not. You will likely *not* listen if you have been getting excellent grades in math and there are people who keep telling you how gifted you are. In other words, the feedback of others must make sense to us in order for us to heed it, and it will not make sense to a person with poor self-insight.

All this means that wisdom relies on our emotions more than we might think. If we are to learn from our mistakes, it helps to *feel* that bad things will happen when we choose foolishly. Wise people are typically capable of considering a particular decision and then imagining or feeling possible consequences. They can *feel* "that would feel horrible," and they don't make that decision. A child who forfeited a favorite toy as a consequence for not listening to a parent will be quicker to listen tomorrow because she remembers the pain of being separated from that toy. Without the emotion of *horrible*, we would all be prone to unwise judgments. People who cannot access these emotions need to learn other ways of making wise decisions.

## LISTEN TO GOD'S PEOPLE

If we are to become wise, we listen—to God and to others. The path for a narcissist follows that same course. Disabilities and weaknesses can make life confusing and relationships difficult, but they cannot, in themselves, keep us from listening to both God and other people. Only a foolish heart can truly make us deaf.

Here are a few selected passages on listening from the book of Proverbs.

> I have called and you refused to listen. (1:24a)

> Whoever listens to me will dwell secure. (1:33a)

> And now, O sons, listen to me,
>     and do not depart from the words of my mouth.
>     (5:7)

> Blessed is the one who listens to me. (8:34a)

> The way of a fool is right in his own eyes,
>     but a wise man listens to advice. (12:15)

Abundant life depends on this. Like young children, we must learn to be "quick to hear" (James 1:19). God's words are life. We must have ears to hear his voice. Yet while the seas and trees seem to have no trouble hearing the words of Jesus, we can be quite deaf. King Solomon, instead, aimed for wisdom. He was an example to us in that he knew our spiritual disability and asked for what was most important: "Give your servant therefore an *understanding mind* to govern your people, that I may discern between good and evil" (1 Kings 3:9). This could be literally translated as a request for a *hearing heart*. It is our great need. The divine King speaks. In response, we hear and act. Our security and life are found in listening to and obeying his word. Our capacity to bless those around us is found in listening to and obeying his word. If a narcissist is to grow, he or she must say, "I need Jesus. I can be rescued by him alone."

## LISTEN, ASK, LEARN

In response, we too aim for humility and listening, and we search for creative ways to help. In this, we are happy to get help from most anyone.

Here are a few useful ideas you might hear.

*Say no to your anger.* Your anger will not help you or the self-absorbed person. It will be distracting and the equivalent of nonsense words if the other person doesn't know what to do with emotions. Instead, you need a calm and measured engagement that invites discussion. In the face of the other person's outbursts, you will want to do *something*, but responding in anger will not help, and identifying your pain might just leave you frustrated. Calm responses are your goal. A conversation will be more productive if there is at least one person in the room who wants to grow in wisdom.

*See the other person as a child.* The self-centered world, the difficulty learning from consequences, the inaccurate self-assessment—these are what we expect from a child. That image can be helpful for you—always their birthday but never growing up. It limits your expectations; it dismantles your assumptions of what you think is understood; it challenges you to communicate in memorable and persuasive ways. Only be careful in how you use it.

The same image applies to those who have a long-term history of addiction: the addiction essentially shields them from the challenges of life that mature us, and the addict is easier to understand as a twelve-year-old rather than a forty-year-old. This is an imperfect analogy, but it can be helpful in your relationship. The benefit is that you will be more patient with the person if your expectations have been adjusted.

Other images include *disabled*, *blind*, and *hard of hearing*. Each image can be bent both toward hard hearts and unusual brains. When you read through the book of Proverbs, you can see the author laboring with questions such as these. How can I help a blind person to see? How can I help a deaf person to hear? How can I help a foolish person who is unable to see the consequences of their actions to learn from their errors? Then watch the wise king's method. He labors to get our attention. He uses vivid images, such as a gold ring in a pig's snout. He uses humor. He doesn't talk too much at one time but leaves room for reflection. He certainly wants his words to catch our attention.

"Look at me, please" is something you might say to a child who is not listening to you. With an adult, you want to speak with respect, but your words might be similar. Your goal is to get their attention and then have them respond to what you said.

"Do you have time to listen? There is something I wanted to talk about." When there is either no response or one that is unrelated to your request, you can repeat it. "When will you have time to listen? I need ten minutes." Notice, you are being more specific and concrete. That can help.

Still no response? Time for humor. You sing, loudly and badly. You bang on the nearest pot. Or you describe your schedule for the day. "Today I have been asked to drag race, with owner's cards going to the winner. Then it is off to the local drug dealer to check out the prices. . . ." When you study the various ways that Proverbs tries to get your attention, you become more creative at getting the attention of others.

And there is a time to be more direct. "I know you are frustrated right now. You can help me to understand what is bothering you, or you can put the frustration aside and we can just move on."

*Do not use "narcissist" and other labels.* Diagnostic labels have their benefits and liabilities. They can help you see certain behaviors. They can also blind you by leading you to believe that everything is a result of the diagnoses, which it is not. For the person who wears the label, the word can be meaningless or offensive. It will not help. The same can be said with words such as arrogance, pride, selfish, entitled and many others. Stick with descriptions: "This is what you do," rather than "This is who you are."

*Practice your own empathy skills.* Empathy is the ability to step into someone's world in a way that the person feels understood. An apparent absence of empathy is what is most difficult about narcissist types. They do not understand either your world *or* their own. In response, you redouble your own efforts to grow in empathy, to which there are many ingredients. Here are three:

1. *Know their story.* When someone is hard to understand, it is helpful to know something of the culture of their family. With narcissism, we might find a history of being spoiled or deprived or parents who were preoccupied in their own selfish worlds and never affected by the good deeds of their children.

Don't expect such discussions to help the person directly though. Those who lack insight are rarely enlightened by their past. They can praise those who were unkind and abusive, while they demean those who were kind and gentle. They usually see past hurts as no big deal and resist our attempts to suggest long-term patterns. But these insights encourage our own patience and kindness.

2. *Assume that they are normal human beings.* Amid all the boasting, entitlement, and "I don't need you or anybody else," expect to find people who want relationship but act in ways that push people away. Expect people who fear failure and, in response, blame others when things go wrong. Expect people who don't know how to deal with or express their struggles. And expect that they do not have the ability to identify these experiences, so the result is meanness. Expect people to be alone and living on that unsettling ground of the opinions of others.

"I think you are saying that you have had a really hard day and I'd love to hear about it even if you would rather avoid it."

3. *Look for good.* When someone is demanding or showing off their greatness for your affirmation, it is hard to see anything good, but empathy looks for the good. If the person is talking about his achievements, try to find one. Look for something good. After hearing complaints about how the world is not serving him as it should, sometimes the good is hard to find. So you pray for help.

And if the complaints and blame keep coming? If you don't know what to say, you probably wouldn't say anything. You might reframe the complaint, "I am the same way—I have plans for the day and then something interferes with my plans." This could open a conversation to how God can use troubles to test our trust in him.

Your goal is to bring together empathy and wisdom. Here is one such response by a wife, spoken with preternatural calm, to her fuming husband. You can almost imagine that she is speaking to a child, yet her language is respectful and inviting.

> "You know, I don't believe a word of that. It's not that I think you are lying. It's just that I know you, and I know how difficult it can be for you to tell me that you miss me. When I'm distracted, like this week, you often feel as if you are unimportant to me. I can understand how upsetting that must be for you. But there is no need to put me down or blame my job. You aren't giving me a chance to care about you when you speak to me that way. . . . I'd like to start the conversation over. How about you?"[9]

She knows her spouse. She knows that emotions and their meanings are elusive to him, so she gives him words that help him. She is specific about what he has done but reminds him, quite clearly, that she *does* care and wants to care. Then she proposes a way to reboot the conversation without it being mired in analysis, which would be asking too much of him. To speak to an immature person like this might not bring instant repentance, but this is a fine example of a skillful response.

*Remember the thing of first importance*. In all this, we hope to speak the truth of Christ with gentleness and kindness and with courage and clarity. We return to our home where we remember what is most important. We "are not [our] own, for [we] were bought with a price" (1 Corinthians 6:20). There, we know that we are not alone, and the Spirit is in these critical details of our lives. Frustration is sure to come, but it gets postponed because you know that *you*—a friend, a family member, a helper— can grow. As God has been patient with you, you extend that patience to others. As God has surprised you with the best of news, you strategize and find help so you too can surprise in the best possible way.

It begins with the Spirit's work in you. You need to be rescued by Jesus, to see yourself in light of God's words, and to live by relying on what Jesus did and the Spirit he gave us. To do that, you return to the good news of Jesus and become persuaded, again, that it truly is good news. Only then can we offer Jesus to others.

## QUESTIONS FOR REFLECTION

1. What questions do you have?

2. What are your tendencies in the face of arrogance or being treated as if you are lesser? How would you like to respond? Our goal is to combine love, humility, boldness, and creativity.

3. What was most helpful for you here? How might it apply to anyone who is difficult to engage?

# ENDNOTES

1. The *DSM* categories also appear in the *International Classification of Diseases* (ICD-11).

2. Henri Nouwen, *Turn My Mourning into Dancing: Moving through Hard Times with Hope* (Nashville: Thomas Nelson, 2001), Kindle version, chap. 1.

3. Adapted from the *Diagnostic and Statistical Manual of Mental Disorders* (*DSM–5*), the American Psychiatric Association, (Arlington, VA : American Psychiatric Association, ©2013.)

4. Judith Herman, *Trauma and Recovery: The Aftermath of Violence—from Domestic Abuse to Political Terror* (New York: Basic Books, 2015), 82.

5. Herman, 109.

6. Elizabeth R. Skoglund, *Bright Days, Dark Nights with Charles Spurgeon in Triumph over Emotional Pain* (Eugene, OR: Wipf & Stock), 69.

7. *DSM–5*

8. M. E. Thomas, *Confessions of a Sociopath: A Life Spent Hiding in Plain Sight* (Crown, 2013), 108, https://books.apple.com/us/book/confessions-of-a-sociopath/id601923525.

9. Wendy Behary, *Disarming the Narcissist* (Oakland, CA: New Harbinger Publications, 2021), 158–59.

# FOR FURTHER READING

These are a sample of the growing literature on how Scripture speaks meaningfully to psychiatric and psychological problems.

### Mental Health and the Bible

- Michael R. Emlet, *Descriptions and Prescriptions: A Biblical Perspective on Psychiatric Diagnoses and Medications*, Greensboro, NC: New Growth Press, 2017

### Anxiety and Panic

- Brad Hambrick, *Burnout: Resting in God's Fairness*, Phillipsburg, NJ: P & R Publishing, 2013 (booklet)
- David Murray, *Reset: Living a Grace-Paced Life in a Burnout Culture*, Wheaton, IL: Crossway, 2017
- Ed Welch, *A Small Book for the Anxious Heart: Meditations on Fear, Worry, and Trust*, Greensboro, NC: New Growth Press, 2019

### Trauma

- Jeremy Lelek, *Post-Traumatic Stress Disorder: Recovering Hope*, Phillipsburg, NJ: P & R Publishing, 2013
- Justin and Lindsey Holcomb, *Rid of My Disgrace: Hope and Healing for Victims of Sexual Assault*, Wheaton, IL: Crossway, 2011
- David Powlison, *Why Me? Comfort for the Victimized*, Phillipsburg, NJ: P & R Publishing, 2003 (booklet)

- Darby Strickland, *Is it Abuse? A Biblical Guide to Identifying Domestic Abuse and Helping Victims*, Phillipsburg, NJ: P & R Publishing, 2020

**Depression**

- Zack Eswine, *Spurgeon's Sorrows: Realistic Hope for Those Who Suffer with Depression*, Scotland, UK: Christian Focus Publishing, 2015
- David Murray, *Christians Get Depressed Too: Hope and Help for Depressed People*, Grand Rapids, MI: Reformation Heritage Books, 2010
- Ed Welch, *Depression: Looking Up from the Stubborn Darkness*, Greensboro, NC: New Growth Press, 2011

**Other General and Specific Topics**

- Michael R. Emlet, *Obsessive Compulsive Disorder: Help for the Struggler*, Greensboro, NC: New Growth Press, 2022 (minibook)
- Tim Keller, *Walking with God through Pain and Suffering*, Westminster, London, UK: Penguin Books, 2013
- Todd Stryd, *Schizophrenia: A Compassionate Approach*, Greensboro, NC: New Growth Press, 2018 (minibook)
- Mark Vroegop, *Dark Clouds, Deep Mercy: Discovering the Grace of Lament*, Wheaton, IL: Crossway, 2019
- Edward T. Welch, *Bipolar Disorder: Understanding and Help for Extreme Mood Swings* (minibook)
- Michael R. Emlet, *Asperger Syndrome: Meeting the Challenges with Hope*, Greensboro, NC: New Growth Press, 2005 (minibook)